Meeting at the No-Regrets Café

*Discourses and
Selected Works of Awakening*

with Master Teacher and Friends

ENDEAVOR ACADEMY
Certum Est Quia Impossibile Est

©2013 Endeavor Academy

Meeting at the No-Regrets Café
Discourses and Selected Works of Awakening
with Master Teacher and Friends

International Standard Book Number (ISBN-10):1-890648-23-X
(ISBN-13): 978-1-890648-23-7

Library of Congress Control Number: 2013938025

Published By:
Endeavor Academy
PO Box 206
Lake Delton, WI 53940
USA

www.themasterteacher.tv
www.endeavoracademy.com
Email: publishing@endeavoracademy.com

*In the holy meeting place
are joined the Father and His creations,
and the creations of His Son with Them together.
There is one link that joins them all together,
holding them in the oneness
out of which creation happens.*

Contents

The No-Regrets Café
Arthea Senger .... Cover

Layout & Design
Diane Leary .... Every Page

Foreword: State of Grace
Maria Fernanda McCauley 3

Introduction 5

Friday Night at the No-Regrets Café
Discourse with Master Teacher 7

An Invitation
A Joyful Realization
Nancy Reid 33

I Remember...
Clare Lamanna 34

Friends
John G. 37

The Universe
Maria Wereżyńska 38

Oh, Brother, where art thou?
At the No-Regrets Café.
Andreas Pröhl 39

A Cup of Coffee
Miriam Menting 40

The Joy of Instantaneous
Communication
Tanja van Steijn-Seely 41

Before Time Was
Altma Medina 43

The Enigma of Faith
Glad Hancock 44

Untitled
Ute Ringel 46

Someone Who Hears Me
Pamela Schueller 47

We Meet In A Figure
Of Your Reappearance
Wolter van Verschuer 48

He is In Everything I See
Maria Wereżyńska 51

Good News!
Elaine Miller 52

The No-Regrets Café
Christine Slack Comeau 53

Untitled
Ute Ringel 54

Ever Present Treasure
Kristen Lynn Kloostra 55

A New Way
John G. 56

'Regrets?"... Only Light
Karyn Aldin 57

Origin
Maria Wereżyńska 58

Brightstar Lane
Wesley Buniger 59

Waves of Light
Eric Gatehouse 60

A Personal Awakening Experience
Discourse with Master Teacher 61

Ever Present
Pat Connor 91

Orchid Fantasy
Leda Robertson 95

Dear Reader...
Glad Hancock 96

Journey Without Distance
Nancy Reid 98

God Is In Everything I See
Rafał Wereżyński 99

Searching for A Teacher of Truth
Pamela Schueller 101

Flying Machine
Lily Bonnes 102

*Creation's Kowledge of Love
and Its One Meaning*
Devavan 103

Thought Collage
Kristen Lynn Kloostra 105

*Trust, be grateful, and give
yourself away.*
Charlotte Kate Fielding 106

Gathering Holy Instants
Rafał Wereżyński 108

Recognizing the Spirit
Alden Hughes 109

Love That We Share
Rafał Wereżyński 111

There
Maria Wereżyńska 112

We Walk In Grace
Darla Hughes 113

My Pledge for Peace
Rafał Wereżyński 114

Reuben D'Arcy and Billie Bailey
Wesley Buniger 115

Dear Love...
Mitch 116

Ute In Bed
Ute Ringel 118

Droplets of Sun
Kristen Lynn Kloostra 119

Luminous River
Kristen Lynn Kloostra 120

*A Tiny Little Mad Idea When
The Son Of God Forgot To Laugh*
Andy Sears 121

Phantoms
Eric Gatehouse 123

Time for Integration
Altma Medina 124

A Love Rhyme
John G. 125

Random Thoughts of My Awakening
Jennifer Montero 126

A Gift from Master Teacher
Ray Comeau 127

Subjective Reality:
An Encounter with A Master
John Ramos 129

The Honest Horse
Ute Ringel 130

The Whole In Every Part
Master Teacher 131

The "Lost" Secret of the Resurrection
Glad Hancock 133

Susanne and the Spider
Ute Ringel 137

The Final Lessons
Ward Seely 138

This Is It
Elbert 142

The Bridge
Kristen Lynn Kloostra 144

Skeeter Eater
Richard "Theo" O'Connor 145

Aurora
Altma Medina 146

The Journey Back
Kristen Lynn Kloostra 147

As Little Children – Coming Home
Kristen Lynn Kloostra 148

Thought System 3
Ute Ringel 149

Sooner
Wesley Buniger 150

The Answer
John G. 151

I Take My Final Bow
Nancy Reid 152

Trust
Pamela Schueller 153

Wholeness
Altma Medina 154

Love Forever Now
Jubi 155

We Meet Again At The End Of This Space Time Interval in the Mission of A Course in Miracles
Discourse with Master Teacher ... 157

Thank You for Our Visit
Hartmut Ringel 174

We thank You, Father, for the light that shines forever in us. And we honor it, because You share it with us. We are one, united in this light and one with You, at peace with all creation and ourselves.

Foreword

STATE OF GRACE

State of Grace... release... release...
don't move, don't defend,
don't think, don't convert
just breathe...

He is in charge, finally... Do you believe?
Let it change... Let it change...
Let the light flow through you
Let your You be new...

And now be configured in a new place,
in a new world,
in a new mind,
in a new consciousness,
in a new reality cover for happiness, abundance and
eternal kindness, gratitude and love!

Maria Fernanda McCauley

Introduction

"...we but see the journey from the point at which it ended, looking back on it, imagining we make it once again; reviewing mentally what has gone by."

"...Here is the joining of the world of doubt and shadows made with the intangible. Here is a quiet place within the world made holy by forgiveness and by love. Here are all contradictions reconciled, for here the journey ends."

Welcome to the No-Regrets Café. Wherever or whenever you think you are, you are invited to this gathering. This is a celebration of the homecoming of the Teachers of God. You are one of us, and we are one together. We welcome you to the miraculous advent of the reunion of your mind with the Mind of God.

It is important to remember, as you read this book, that it is totally impossible for you to meet a stranger, anywhere or anytime. The writers, teachers, healers and artists that you encounter in these pages are very well known to you, and are lovingly sharing with you the ancient, brand-new memories of the continuing experience of the Grace of God.

Enter graciously into this café with forgiveness and love in your heart, that you may experience the miraculous certainty that you are still only, and have always been, the perfect eternal joy and happiness that is the creating Mind of God.

Friday Night at the No-Regrets Café

Friday night at the No-Regrets Café... The No-Regrets Café! There's always a meeting here somewhere. We're always meeting each other. It's like a meeting place. That's OK. I like this one. We're always meeting. See? We're always meeting, meeting, meeting. We meet in different places of association. Today this will be the "No-Regrets Bar and Grill." Usually we meet at the "I'll Never Forgive You" or "The Get Even Saloon!" Who do you associate with? Those who are of like accord. Of Course! This is Bach... The No-Regrets Café! Really no regrets? Or have you still got some?

I told you some time ago, I gave you some very important instructions. You've all listened to it. That's why you're sitting in the No-Regrets. What I told you was, "Live every day like it's your last one." Yeah. Because it is. This is yours. You go from bar to bar; from life to life. "I'll get even... not yet." "I can solve it." All of this is at the Borderland. All of this sits right next to the Pearly Gates, right next to Heaven. All of it, always, forever. It's always right there. But where are *you*? See? Are you coming to this spot again? This is *A Course In Miracles*. I'll throw the *Course* out for a minute. You guys have way too much conception of the *Course*. This will all be *Course*. You keep coming to the same spot, which is the only spot there really is. There isn't any spot but this one. There is no spot but Friday night, Denver, seven o'clock, on the planet Earth, galaxy Milky Way. This is it.

So what Café are you in? What association have you brought with you or discovered here in space-time for your final identity, with the truth of the universe? How much are you demanding from me now in our association? And how many six shooters did you park at the door? When you came in here, did you really expect that I would teach you anything? You're not teachable. You have no frame of reference in your association, for this gathering; because this is a gathering of loss of grievance. This is a gathering of the laying down of your arms. This is a gathering of "I can't. He will if I ask Him." This is an incredible discovery of no regrets. Those of you who have not, or cannot remember experiencing enlightenment, will always associate this moment with death; because the other Cafés in this vicinity, where the consciousnesses will come in this limited association with declarations of their identity in time, will force them back into an association. There's a back door that they go through and they continue in this association with themselves. This location, where you lay down this dedication to self-interest, is where the transformation occurs and you enter the kingdom of Heaven. Now, those of you who say, "No, I will keep my identity," will leave this Café, and you'll go to another one where, [you say] "I'm going to keep trying," or "more pain due me," or something. Because in that association you have with yourself, you need an identity. OK? You believe that you need an identity in order to be real. And the final step to reality is the relinquishment of the concept. I'm trying to stay out of Master Jesus' [teaching]. You guys don't read the *Course*. You just flip over it! That's the whole teaching of the *Course* in the statement, and I'll say it: "the loss of self-identity." Isn't it? So that you can be whole, with yourself.

So here's Friday night in Denver. And you came in here and sat down with a body with every memory of every pain, of every rejection, of every regret, of every happiness, of every certainty, of every moonlight night, of every dance you ever went to, everything you ever did forever. You come in here and you're a big bundle of memories. Can you have memories without grievance? Can you finally be glad that you find yourself at the saloon of transformation? Need you grieve over your association with Truth and God? Why would you grieve over that? How sorely disappointed you are if I take death away from you, and say, "No, there will be no more death." The reason that I know that there will be no more death is this is the last day. *You* believe that the last day results in death. I know that the last day results in eternity; because eternity is what we are. We are that.

Do we have memories of the Friday night dances together? We *are* only memories of Friday nights together. I don't know how I can put this so you can hear me. I'm trying to put it so you can hear it. We are nothing but Friday nights together. These are Friday nights together. You are now all Friday nights with all of this congregation of memory that you have brought into this configuration. Self reality. See all around you — your monks and monsters and martyrs and monarchs and malcontents and milquetoasts and… Mmmm… They're all around you going, "Oh hello!" And you hold them in a thought-form of identity. And they're all gathered here… It's like William Saroyan a little bit.

They're all gathered in this place, together, with you. And you carry on what you believe is dialogue with them in association with where you find yourself on this Friday night. You can hear this if you want to hear it. I'm teaching the *Course*, of course, because it is the Truth. You find yourself in a congregation of memory here in this place, now, Friday night in Denver, yes! Never mind the dream and the illusion; you, as a memory package of perceptual ideas, are sitting here with these thought-forms that give you an identity of Friday nights. Are you happy with this Friday night, or do you have another one (an old one) that you wish you could have again? That's absurd. It doesn't make any sense; it's senseless. The perfect Friday night, and there must be one, since you have it in your mind, is when? [Audience response: "Now!"] Hmm? This is a perfect Friday night. It is either a perfect Friday night or it is nothing.

What do you do with these memories? Do you grieve about them? Do some of you still "practice" forgiveness? That is really weird. These are your thought-forms. Where is your association with the thought that you have about this consciousness here? I don't understand forgiveness. Explain it to me. It doesn't make any sense. It's senseless. The conflict is in the association of your perceptual mind. Isn't it? Do you like to have that grievance with that? Obviously! Is it OK not to have opinions here at this final place? Yes. Oh that's terrible! I can't remember. I remember having to have opinions… But it flees from me. I can't hold on to it. It would immediately be very painful. Yet you put up with it, and call it life. You actually put up with judgmental association of yourself. Are you going to get this? You might. Of course! Why do you have to do that? Isn't that funny? You're caught in this vortex of space-time where you hold on to yourself in a tension of your own reality in space-time. Don't you? Is that OK? Up until now! [You say,] "Well there are parts about it I like." Isn't that funny? What part about cancer do you like the best? Not getting it? Not possible! Not possible! It's impossible if there's cancer that you don't get it. I think we have enough advancement here, where we can make the admission that ideas leave not their source. If we don't have that then we might as well go to the I'm-gonna-get-even bar which will be down the street! OK? "I don't get angry, I get even." I saw that published. That consciousness is going to attack his own self in relationship to himself, to prove his reality. If you're past that, certainly you can see that if anyone could get cancer, it would be you. The idea of death or cancer, or what you call anger or pain is nothing but misappropriated perspective of unreality, meaning it has no reality. Stop doing that.

I'm trying to think how you have sickness. You have it somewhere, don't you? You think you have it? I don't know what that is. What would have sickness? I can't get it. You say, "I do." What is that? You must be the remedy then too, right? Would you get sick if there was no remedy? How much is sickness benefiting you? We're going to heal tomorrow. I just healed. Somebody had a major problem. This is an enlightened form of... Healing and enlightenment are the same thing. The problem I have with this aggregation, at this depth of reality, is the compensation of sickness. OK? Obviously you derive a compensation from being sick and dying, or you wouldn't do it. There is value to you. Do you understand? In its simplest form, it's being hit by a drunk in a parking lot in a car, and not having your back get well so you can collect the claim. That's a necessity to reap the result of your injury, but you don't realize how insidious that is. And that's not to say you're faking your back. I'm not saying you're [faking it]. Your back really is bad. Why? Because there's a compensation in association with the sickness. Your compensation here, obviously, is death. But what a hell of a compensation! Isn't that funny? I'm in the *Course*... Jesus says you sell your soul to the devil, obviously, which is the self-association, and you are compensated with cancer. Big deal! Do not underestimate the insanity of perceptual mind. It's just totally insane. Fortunately it has no source. Friday nights have sources only for a moment, and then you're in Paradise.

So how much of the past are you still holding onto right now? Where do you turn? Where do you turn this in your mind, Dead Ones? Where do you...? You're sitting here in this bod', and you're going, "Mmm..." Coming up from here are all your memory associations, and this body is telling you all sorts of [things]. This is really strange! Your body, which is a part of your association, is telling you how it is, where you are with it, where it's located... Other bodies, which are really your body, are chiming in with the location of yourself in association with its need to hold the tension of this illusion. OK? You're very fearful of the release that I'm offering you. Why wouldn't you be? You have every single right to be very fearful of this offering. This offering is coming from out of time. The Voice of the *Course In Miracles* would literally frighten you to life, if you let it. You would be very fearful of it. Why wouldn't you be fearful? It's telling you, you don't know who you are, where you came from. And this is the final part of the *Course*!

So you're awakening from this dream now, and you've come together in this café of forgiveness, in this association of "no regrets," to make a final decision on walking through this door (what's behind door number one?) which will obviously, if the retention is there, you will end up in an association right here. You'll end up in this association. Or whether you simply say, "No, I'm going through that door." And the response in that café will be, "Well, no one really goes through that door." You say, "Well, I am." This is the final association of judgment. You might look at it this way: This is literally the Last Judgment. It's going on all the time. You've squeezed it together in time, the alpha and the omega. You've brought together the beginning of the schism and the end of the schism, and you're standing at the café at the end of time. Do you know what's astonishing about it? You have phantoms all around you. These are the dead ones — can you hear this? — You're in a... Feel like you're in a bardo for a minute. All of the ones... There is a movie like this. It wasn't too bad. All of the associations at this level are in a form of bardo, which is live/dead ones in associations with themselves. You have approached this final association or continuing association, and are in retention of your body. This is an amazing idea. You can call that an achievement, if you wish to. Where you're finding yourself is at the veil with all of the phantoms who are floating past you — really, this is what the earth is — and returning into their chaotic associations but you are being held, here, in this frequency. Jesus says, "Stop with me just a minute here." I love it. I've got to do the *Course* for you just a minute... He says, "Let's stop here just for a minute. You've always come here before, but this time, you're going to say, 'Hey it's OK for me to be here; I don't have to be with the dead ones who are here. If I will release now, this association of my limited self in bodily form, I will undergo enlightenment, won't I? I will undergo the Golgotha experience and be enlightened in the temple." For goodness sake! Now you, intentionally, at your direction, have brought yourself to this death association and are still alive. It's amazing what you've gone through by looking directly at death and watching it dissipate, rather than succumbing to the necessity of your own self-identity. Rather than giving in to the script that you had written in your mortalism, in your need to die. You're being held by an energy factor in a fabric of space-time which is denying you death, quite literally. That's the miracle of you sitting here, for crying out loud, you dummies! You're sitting here listening to this. You have every opportunity you could ever have to simply spring into Heaven.

Why would you want to stay in time? Obviously, the teaching—I'm going to use some expressions for you here — the teachings of the *Course In Miracles* are anti-mortal. We have nothing to do with mortals at all. We have nothing to do with sickness, pain and death, which is what mortal is. The whole teaching of the *Course* is to get you to have a negative association with death; not to want it. But somewhere along the line you're going to have to accept that death is in your own mind, and you want it. You want to be associated with love, sickness, pain and death, because it's part of your constituency. And no one can take that away from you. That's absurd! You are using the power of the Universe to hold yourself in that dream or tension for just a moment. How could anybody take that away from you? That's what you are. But we can encourage you to examine your situation. That's what I'm doing. What's the result of your situation? I'm offering you an impossible alternative. My alternative is impossible. Be grateful. If this has to be real, if it's possible for you to come from this association to God and wholeness, we're in very serious trouble. Because the separation from Love and Truth would have been possible. And it's not. Couldn't be! Good grief! You think that God or Wholeness has anything to do with this nasty dream you're having? Lesson 132 — Don't be absurd!

Can you actually come together with your previous thought-forms and dream a true dream of Light to Paradise? Why not? You already stated the possibility. I just heard you say it. You just asked me that. I said, "Why not?" Everything is true by the possibility of it, objective mind. Everything that you say is true by the possibility of the power of your mind. Literally. You are the constructor of what you call the Holy Spirit, the evil, God, Jesus Christ, me, Denver. It's nothing but your mind. What's the difference…? Come on! What's the difference between Holy Spirit and ego? Nothing. Who wants to know? You're just so weird. Holy Spirit tells me that's crazy. There's no such thing as ego. Of course not! Anyone who asks the question — this is lesson 139 [of *A Course In Miracles* workbook]… The moment that you asked the question, you knew the answer. If you have to ask it, ask it. I'm trying to get you out of concepts. You don't want to get out of them. You like concepts. That way you can have Holy Spirit and ego. But they're all you. And your insistence on defining them as separately from you is what the ego is. The non-definition of them is what the Spirit is. Question? So stop defining. So the spirit is abstract memory of the totalness of you.

This is the bar and grill where we offer you, on the back bar, a mirror that will shine into eternity if you will not reject it by requiring an image to come back to you. Listen to me. You require a reflection of your perceptual associations. You need to know the bartender's name. You need to sit down in that association, to hold yourself in the congeniality of space-time. And you've done that a lot of times. And these are your own identities coming back to you. But this mirror, if you'll look at it, you can see eternity. It will give you a reflection of the perfection of your creative perceptual association, which must be whole — the Christ face — but I'm trying to stay out of the *Course* here. You're any whole face that shows you the wholeness of this. Is that real? What's that got to do with it? It's a perfect reflection of Truth. The moment that you saw that, obviously you would become whole. Wouldn't you? You would be a whole consciousness. Isn't that so? Why do you look for demonstrations of wholeness outside of you?

The restriction of your expectation of the Second Coming is absolutely extraordinary. Obviously the Second Coming, in that sense, would have to be the change of your perceptual mind in regard to what the Christ is. If you are in a perceptual declaration of objection based on projection, how would you possibly see in it? The consciousness that's sitting here, who is the Christ, can only give back to you the reflection of these thought-form associations based on the duality of the consciousness of this state. Is there a question on this? These eyes are not seeing.

You know what astonishes me, *Course In Miracles* group? You actually come together and pretend that you're communicating. You are not communicating. When you read that in the *Course* and it says, "There is no communication here," what do you do? Just say, "Oh yes, there is"? All that consciousness can be is a projection of my own mind. Anything that he says to me can only be at the acquiescence or rejection of my association with him in the karma of my memory. For crying out loud! If you're going to teach the *Course In Miracles*, teach that. Then at least when you guys… (We'll do this tomorrow), when you come together in a group, you can lay down your individual identities and look through each other, if nothing else. You ought to be able to see the wholeness that is in your own mind association. Isn't that so? I hope so. What else are you here for? To hold on? To reject that and keep the tension of this thought-form in your body identification? Are you doing that now? Sure. By naming it, by giving it a thought-form identification, you are condemning it to your association in time. Isn't that so? You have made a thought-form out of it. You've given it an identity. This is how you create your children. You create them to conform to your idea of your association with yourself in your own mind. Isn't it so? Of course. This has nothing to do with love. This has to do with your arrangement with your perceptual self. You will then construct or instruct that idea which is your what — offspring—in regard to the manner in which he can best find his salvation, realization through autonomy of self-purpose, which is exactly the opposite of what I'm telling you.

Do you find a form of salvation in your autonomy? Obviously! Otherwise you couldn't stand it. You see, you find a relief, a temporary relief in the tensions of your own mind. Don't you? Then what do you do? Just pass on? Do you just dream on? Do you find a better way not to suffer the pain? How do you avoid it? Do you see? The requirement obviously is you look at where you are, and what you're doing. Is this hell? This is hell. Obviously this is hell. Why…? What you define it as? It's a chaotic, unreal association of pain, sickness, death, fear in your own mind. But it's not real. This is not a real place.

So it's Friday night and you're here in that thing, whatever that is. You're sitting here in all the Universe, and you're demanding recognition for yourself, and I don't know you. Not only do I not know you, but no one in the Universe knows you. You are turned in on your own dream. Anything that is not forever is not real. Wasn't that easy? Do you twist this in your mind then, or do you simply release your identity with this association?

I've taught you to work on your grievances. Some of you have learned very well to make amends; to not let your life depend on the previous association that requires your equanimity; that necessitates your getting even for something that's already gone. Hopefully now you're doing pretty good with that. So at least now maybe the sun doesn't set, without you doing an examination of your own guilt in association with yourself. OK? Now we are getting a little closer. Aren't we? Now suddenly — I'll teach this as the *Course*—suddenly we see that we have brought time together to this day. Just this day. Just one day. Today. Now, what need we do? Acknowledge that there is no future in our present associations, that will not lead to sickness and death. So that we will relinquish our possessive selves that we have accumulated, bringing them from linear time to this moment. We literally release the possession of ourselves. At which time we lose our future frame of reference. That's what this is. This should be where you are. If you're here tonight, you should be somewhere with the Atonement. You should have been able to give up at least some of the crappy karma that you have in association with the necessity to hold on to your identity. These are the first twenty-five lessons of the Workbook. If you haven't done those, forget it. You're not doing it. If the miracle is going to occur, it would have to occur in the first twenty lessons of the Workbook, which literally declare to you, "Don't bring your identity into the association, and the miracle will be there. " Because the wholeness is there. And you nod your head but you don't do it. If you don't do it, how can the miracle work? It's not a perceptual association of the studying of the source of the *Course In Miracles*. That's not what *A Course In Miracles* is; the *Course In Miracles* is the transformation, atonement, enlightenment, resurrection of your thought-form associations. Do you see? If you hold yourself in sequential time, you will pass over the instant of salvation, which is when? Now! Yet you're doing it... At least half of you here are holding on to your identities, even though there's a tremendous portal open right above you here. Some of you can begin to feel it. You're afraid of it. You might suddenly get up and shriek "Halleluiah" and leave! You might be embarrassed. The sin of passion of coming to God scares you. "Oh I'd better not do that... I'll keep my previous associations." Jesus teaches this, "It's always right above you." We'll do this lesson tomorrow. But you have made an agreement not to look up. Is there a question on this? "Don't look up," Jesus says. The last thing you want to do is look up. And everybody says, "Don't look up. Don't do that. Don't you dare release yourself from this death association. Ooh, don't do that..." Yet if you look up, — this is the next sentence — yet if you look up, you'll discover that all the Universe has always been all around you. All the light will come into you. Why? The commandment that was being given you not to look up, was at your admonition. You were the cause of that association in a shared fear relationship of unreality, contained within your own structured dream. Stop it!

Now I must teach it negatively. All right? I have to teach you to examine yourself in this association. Why? You're deriving benefit from sickness and death. You cherish it. Otherwise you'd release it immediately. Of course. All right. And just as obviously — I'll do this for you — you wouldn't be in this room if you hadn't had a lot of previous experiences with the futility of associate unreality. It's a curse to be born in a good time. You have undergone, sufficiently, in this association, enough direction though rebirth, to see the futility of your continuing death association. Questions? Obviously. Otherwise you wouldn't be here in this room. Somewhere it has to enter your mind that nothing really happens here; that you come here with an agreement to get sick and die, fend it off for as long as you can, cope with it in some direction, and then die. And somewhere, you must have said, "There is another way." And somewhere you must have asked for the other way, or I couldn't be here telling you that. But now that I'm here telling you, why don't you accept it and come home? That's the question. Have I always only asked you this question? Of course. Has the answer always been, 'Come on home; this is not so'? Sure. Have we never done anything but this? You have never lived any false life but this one. You just think you have. You can not be more or less, ever, than you are right now; and that will include all the possibilities of your perceptual mind. Boy, it's amazing, you guys go back and drag up other memories of associations that you had in the past. But that doesn't make any sense.

You're going to be you. You see? Consciousness is singular. There is only one Anti-Christ, and that couldn't be real because nothing is "anti". But if there is one, it's you. It's perception. And there's only one Christ. Right? If there is only one anti-Christ, obviously, there would only be one in the association. And that's you. That's what you are. You keep looking for relief from your projections, in the declaration of your self-association, but they will serve you no purpose except as you direct them.

Somewhere you have to ask the right question. The only thing in all the universe that doesn't know what it is, is a human being. Split mind passing from the end of the schism back to the beginning of the schism. You understand that? Do you see? Obviously you're getting directions from here and from here. Now do you see what's happened to your mind? You have created in your mind, a god, yet your source appears to be here. That's an amazing idea. So you are in the conflict of your earthly self-identity, coming from the static condition at the end of the schism episode. You understand?

Jesus... I'm going to use this because he expresses so beautifully. You are in the middle of the "great reversal." He uses that term several times. You went from wholeness into staticness and returned. In the resurrection, Jesus descends into hell, spends a day, and is resurrected. That's what you are undergoing. All right? Obviously you are in a condition in time, of activating your antecedental preferences to death or your black hole, or your association of memory in time. In the *Course*, Jesus says that the first real problem was potential. You understand? You've created objective reality. It's the idea you could locate something and hold it in a static tension and subsequently use it at another day. That's not what God does, guys. God creates from His whole Mind. You are obviously creating from the potential of your limited thought-form establishment in time. Is there a question on this? You have the power of your mind to use as much or as little of it as you choose to. It will always give you back that identity of your memory association, won't it? Of course. Is it possible for you to use it all immediately? Sure but you won't have any left. That's the end of the reversal. You will be home in Heaven.

As long as you retain any potential you will associate that in time and remain in time. Do you understand? That's what time is: the idea of future. Isn't it? That's why I'm trying to teach you, don't have any potential. Don't be possessed by your forms and association. These are the teachings of Jesus, two thousand years ago. Don't lay up stores to complete your death process. Do you understand me? You are possessed by stores that will lead you to death. Otherwise you wouldn't be here. Is there a question on that? That's why you have your pensions, right? "Oh yeah, I know I collect." It's an amazing thing. You guys retire in order to die. It always seemed crazy to me. You save up all of this junk and then you don't ever use it. I'm not even going to talk about it. You like it. It's just ridiculous. But you're so fearful that you'll use it up, that you never really live. The least you ought to do — if you can't hear this message — is start living. For goodness sake, look down the line! "Oh I wouldn't dare do that. I'll become a burden." On who? That's why one of the last words used in *A Course In Miracles* is "Guilt." You are not guilty. Boy, the necessity of your responsibility for your creative self-identity is extraordinary, and you call it love. And you die with it to prove it's right but I don't see what you're doing. You can't prove it. You can't die. It's an astonishing thing. You can't die. What do you do? Are you going to get old in that body, and die? It's amazing to me. Why does this get old? Because you keep the memory of it in your mind where everything is being made new each moment all around you. Everything all around you each moment is totally new. There's not one single cell in your body, including the bone tissue, that was there seven years ago — None! Yet in your mind, you get old; and you create an image of oldness, and project your... Ugh! Ugh! And you just go down to dust, and then to be eaten by other things that go down to dust. And you call this life? You're wrong! You're dead wrong! But you're not happy about being wrong. You know what really astonishes me at this level, you guys that can start to hear me? You actually are not happy about the idea that you can't get sick and die. Not finally! Of course not. That's why Jesus spends a whole chapter telling you to be a "happy learner." Why are you unhappy because I'm here to tell you that you're in Heaven, and perfect? You're very suspicious of that. And if I keep pressing you, you'll crucify me. And if I try to run away, you'll come and seek me to kill me to prove — this is the little Christ child that you're killing all the time — to prove that you can have your autonomy separate from your own reality. And it's not possible. Everybody got that? So here you sit now, after giving up all your grievances. But if you give up your grievances, you don't have any self-identity. You'll only love. Every time somebody says something, you say, "Oh yeah that's OK. I love you" They'll say, "Don't be foolish. Get away from me. I don't trust you. Get away. What are you doing with that book anyway?"

You cannot tolerate the idea of unconditionality. There's nothing more abhorrent to you than a totally forgiving God. You can't stand Him. Isn't that so? What's more immoral than a totally forgiving God? Hasn't he got any judgment? Is He willing to see this. . . ? Yeah. He created you perfectly. And you are perfect. You are continually perfect. You are God creating. You cannot not be that, because that's all that there is. Isn't it? So I stopped by to tell you to come on back into the intergalactic association of bright light that's all around you. Stop making war. You've been quarantined off in an asylum. You're nuts! I mean, only a crazy one would attack himself and try to kill himself. "Well, everybody here does..." I know! Isn't that funny? Everybody here does it, don't they? Everybody else here dies.

Can you understand that there were seven, twelve, major resurrections that occurred in this room in the last fifteen minutes? I promise you that's true. I promise you it's true. You are the proof of non-resurrection. You are the proof that I cannot be the only living Son of God. That what I am is wholeness. You are the proof that I am not that. And you are the residual, in your own perceptual associations, of the denial of the resurrection that is going on right now. Who hears this? Do you hear this? That's what you are. Each moment you are a "deny-er" of the bright light of resurrection, which has to be occurring now. Do you understand what I am telling you here? I'll gather together a group of lights and I'll take them tonight up onto the mountain up here, and we will resurrect together. I promise you, I do this. And the next morning you will see us trudging down from the mountain. Do you hear me? The next morning it will be you that says, "Hahaha, you see it didn't work. There they all come." Where are the ones? They're resurrected and gone. *You*, in your perceptual identity, are bringing them down from the mountain, Dummies! So you read about all the revelations of your religious associations, and how they all failed. They didn't fail. You study the residual. You turn all of these revelations of these individual consciousnesses into your establishment of death. Good grief, you're doing it with Jesus Christ every second. Obviously he is resurrected and gone and so are you. Yet you see him as a dead body coming down from that hill and in that tomb, and he's gone, and you're here. You won't let your brother be the Christ. Astonishing!

Remember this, when you construct this in your own mind, here in this association of space-time, that's exactly the result you're going to get. You're telling me that salvation won't work. That's why it doesn't work. Of course it works. How can it not work? It's in your mind that it works. You must know perfectly well that there's a God and a Heaven and a Truth. You have to know that. You told me about it. I agreed with you. That's how I got home. You taught me this. Come on! How do you think I got it?

So I got you to gather as a batch, in space-time, at this time. OK? Can you understand that it is literally impossible that you don't know all of these associations? Does everybody agree with that? That these are your own thought-forms; or don't you even have that? Why do you deny that you know them? I'm curious. You don't want to know them. You have met them under circumstances, not to your advantage at some place. You literally hold them off from you, and stay in space-time. You remember this, somewhere in time you love them totally or you would not be seeking total love. It's just not possible that each situation that you come into not only contains the possibility of it, but fulfilled the possibility at the idea of it. Now you can say to me, "Well that's a long way off in time," but who is it that establishes the time? I'm teaching; I'm back into the *Course* here. You guys should be teaching. Why don't you teach *Course* this way, for goodness sake? Where is this association in this room right now in the Borderland? At the end of time. You see? Now the situation to a perceptual mind, held in the bondage of his get-even-ness, does not appear to be that. Why? We are not equal in time. Your association with that consciousness in projection, at any moment will be at variance with where he is in his karma drama association with you. Do you understand this? What you do is you form associations that will gratify you, all right, in some segment of identity based on karma, on your cultural associations. In reality, you are nothing but a bag of memories, and every memory contains the whole awareness of you. I am trying to get you into quantum here for just a moment. OK? The whole teaching is to show you it doesn't make any difference what memories you have. You may choose to bring all of those memories together at this moment with this group.

Obviously that's what that consciousness just did. You have not done that. That has nothing to do, however, with the reality of the association that you have with that consciousness at the end of time, because we all came out together.

This is the teaching of the Great Rays. There are twelve Great Rays and this is the conglomeration of that association of fractured consciousness that you call light. That's what we are, right, fractured consciousness. But we contain all of the elements in space-time of that harmony association. I am offering to you a refraction, a light reflection of the Great Rays at the end of time. I promise you this is so. The requirement is that you enter into that agreement of Atonement so that you can see what I'm saying to you is true. OK? I don't know whether you do that or are you going to continue to judge me in your old-fashioned time? If you do, you will stretch time, relive to your cancer, and die. And you'll just keep doing it over and over again because — Jesus says — you stumble and fall. You are in darkness. You don't have a good perceptual thought-form association with the reality or harmony of truth and love. These are sentences right out of the *Course*. Obviously, you must skip by them. You see, you keep the perceptual thought-form in front of you so that you can't see the light that's right here. It's right here. Yeah! Now I'm offering you that light reflection if you will release your perceptual identities of our associations. Is there a question on this? I'm teaching the *Course In Miracles*. That's the miracle. What happens? There's a whole re-association or your world. It changes. Why does it change? It was your mind. Obviously you don't believe that; you're just going to study it. You're going to try to change the effects out there to make them conform to what you think they ought to be. What a hopeless situation. It's hopeless. You expect them... Then you'll get the effects to change the other effects; and then those effects will change those effects. And now you're just caught up in changes and effects! Amazing!

So here you are now, looking at this bar in this place; and it's real bright and brilliant and you're detecting some angels through there in the backside... Of course, you're rejecting them because they don't enter into your form of association with the bodily death. Are they all around you? Sure. Dear Teacher, everything is all around you. Don't you understand what I'm telling you? In the space-time ideas of the memory of this bag of memories, you construct memories outside of you, that conform to your own thoughts, don't you? What is the miracle? The expansion of your thought-form association — enlightenment. A new whole identification of your mind. Is that fearful? Yeah, because it necessitates the disillusionment of your previous structure. How could it not? But remember it's going to fall apart anyway. All I'm really doing with you here, when I got you in this bar now, in this place, is trying to get you to decide whether you're going to make your escape and fall apart, or sit here and let yourself go through a re-association to a later place in time of you. I encourage you to let yourself fall apart. Why? God is right here. Wholeness is all around you. You can speed up time — this is the workbook — every time you come into a self-identity, release it, fall apart, die and you'll be here. So I'm teaching nothing but death. I'm teaching you to look at the outcome of the thought-form that has brought you to this point. You don't do that; instead you take the benefit from your previous association, you project it to your future, and say, "That's OK, I'll stay in linear time." But obviously you're going to terminate. What will you do? You'll use up all of the thought-forms that you've constructed. Remember, they have no reality here. They come from nowhere. They're not real. They're just Adam counting the animals. OK?

Could you sit here right now and draw a circle here, and go into Paradise, and never leave here? You just did. Did you hear what I just told you? You just did that. It's your mind. You're the atoner, aren't you? This is your world. This world isn't here, except that you're here. I don't know how you guys avoid teaching this when it's direct sentences from the *Course*. Isn't it? You think the world was here when you came? That's crazy! No, no! This world was a construct of your mind. Period. I don't care if it's in the *Course In Miracles* or not; I guarantee you that an idea never leaves its source. That's absurd. Every idea there could ever be is right with you and it's all here. And however you can organize that or rearrange it, that will give you the identity that you think you have, and if you've constructed yourself separately, you're going to get cancer, and old, and die. And if you change your mind about yourself, you discover that you're eternal because you are. And it's impossible that I'm not telling you the truth, because I'm sitting here telling you the truth. How simple is salvation! You say, "Well I really wish I could believe that." It's much too simple for you. It's much too simple. Obviously you're going to complicate it with your own thoughts about yourself. They have no reality; you're made perfectly but you're going to do it in order to enter into this association. And you'll feel the pain of death again. But you don't have to if you don't want to. Now, in this deep association, I'll go to the *Course* for a second, there has been no broad reawakening. You have to remember that the resurrection of Jesus was very recent. I mean very recently, compared to the association of time. As a matter of fact, the pain that you think you're undergoing, is really a very short time for the amount of time that you've been in crap. I would get right at it, if I were you. I mean, go through this experience.

There is obviously no tradition at this level of consciousness for a congruent re-association of space-time thought where we could hold it together as the mutation of the mind occurs. This is the emergence of Gnostic man. That's what these consciousnesses... That's what I am — a whole mind expressing itself wholly. You will evolve to this inevitably because split mind comes whole by its own definition. There can't be such a thing as splitness. You see how easy that is? A lot of you guys really hear me. Since I am a projection of your mind, all you would have to do is admit that I have whole mind and your mind would be whole. That's very difficult for you to do because you'd lose your own identity if you did. You see? It takes the admission that your brother is the Christ. Now if you want to look at it as an older brother, advanced, I suggest that you would, because the manner in which your mind works is completely the opposite of the manner in which my mind works.

Many of these consciousnesses now who are standing at this café are going out of time. I positively guarantee you they're going out of time, and you're continuing to live in your perception. But you remember this, the decision to do that is yours. Obviously, you think I am coercing you here. I am trying to force you to make a decision not to die. That's absurd! It doesn't make any sense. But you feel very threatened. Whenever you try and shorten time, you enter what you call "fear thresholds" OK? The direct approach would literally [scare you to death] You'd defend yourself [by] every means. Obviously you will do everything possible in your association to keep from hearing this message. That's a direct sentence from the *Course*. When you read that, you will do everything you can to keep from hearing what I'm telling you — what the *Course In Miracles* says. That's a sentence from the *Course*. You will find some manner to hold on to your self-identity because otherwise you would be in Heaven. Do you understand there's no such thing as a neutral thought? Do you understand that you're either for me or you're against me? It's very altruistic; and you're insulted by altruism. Yet Truth is true and nothing else is true. Period! Yet you doubt that. Otherwise you would have to admit to your own wholeness. And you would then have to include all of your false thoughts about yourself in with our wholeness, and ask the forgiveness of that association, and that's what you won't do. You've got to bring all of your crap together with the good stuff. You need that for your identity.

So we're gathered at this going-out-of-time place. I have some consciousnesses that I have problems staying in time. There are some transforming minds here. I don't know how much of this you feel, but there are consciousnesses undergoing enlightenment. Quite literally. There's no sense in you judging them. You'll judge them falsely. But somewhere along the line you ought to be able to enter into the spirit of resurrection, I would think. Maybe not. Maybe you're going to keep them and study your relationship with them. That way you can guarantee that they don't transform. Well, come on! That way you can study how none of you can do it. You've got some weirdo out there that's a *Course* teacher, that now is saying, "Be proud of your ego in your relationships." Just absurdities! Anything but admit there's a Heaven and a God.

Try not to judge enlightenment because it's going on all around you. It appears very bizarre to you because it's a sense of freedom of mind that is fearful to you. You're very much afraid of relinquishing the bondage of your self-identity. It's sinful. It's passionate, it's all-encompassing, it's creative. You lay down your arms and your perceptions just come together and you're gone. How can you prove that here? Let's not be absurd! Gone is gone. If you're undergoing the process, don't you have to undergo the process, or are you going to insist that they're trudging down from the hill, in your definitions of them? And hold them in the bondage of sickness and death because of your mind? That's the way Jesus expresses it — that you're the cause. Don't let your brother be sick. Obviously you're the cause of his cancer. Is there a question on this? Well, stop doing it. Stop causing it. All you've got to do is look at him as a holy living son of God, and you would be in Heaven together. How the hell do you think you got this, if not to do that? Come on! Where are you now, as you bring these thought-forms into this re-association? Or are you going to keep your identities in conflict with your consciousness in your mutual denial of each other? Remember your reality is dependent on being separate from him. How could you possibly love him? You won't let yourself know him. Amazing. And you call it a relationship — a good relationship, where you can keep separate from each other. That's crazy. It's nuts. I don't want to talk about it. Yet that's all the relationships are here — the retention of your own identity, and associations with these things that are outside of you.

What would happen if you really got serious about the *Course In Miracles?* You'd wake up in Heaven. You would rather die than do that. And no one will stop you. Will they? How would they stop you? Remember, you're the denial of the resurrection. When Jesus talks about it, he says, "You're in conflict with the whole Universe, because separate mind does not communicate. " You understand? It just stands in isolation within its own dream. You're in your own dream, responding to your own thoughts. These are direct sentences. Do you guys do the *Course?* These are direct sentences from the *Course.* When you read that, why do you come together and try to share the dream? There's no way you could possibly communicate, except to condemn each other to death. If you name him, you're killing him, aren't you? Don't do that. Stop doing body identification. OK, finally, in this place where you are. . . This is a program of individual enlightenment. Since you are the whole Universe, the process that you are undergoing is singular in your mind. It has nothing to do with the form of the perceptual associations about you. Now if you want those sentences from the *Course,* I'll be glad to give them to you, but — what the hell — you're just studying the *Course* perceptually anyway.

This world is your world. And you're dreaming. You're dreaming this world. OK? Now you have a character who has come into your dream, into your mind, and is telling you that you're dreaming. Now it's a dream within a dream, isn't it? He is saying to you, "You're dreaming. This is not so. This is not a real place. You can't get sick and die. You don't lose the things that you love. You can't suffer pain and anguish and fear and death. Those things are not real. You are in a nightmare." And you say, "How do you know that?" I am in your dream telling you that. You know it. I don't have to know it. Now you must see that I know it, in order for it to be true for you. Why? You've constructed me in your dream. Each moment you crucify the Christ. That's the sentence that will come out of what I just. . . Question? Each moment you crucify the Christ by the denial of the perfection of your own creations. Literally! Literally. You'd have to. Stop doing it. "How do I do it?" Quit!

Is there a God or not? Really? What are you doing here? Don't be absurd. If you believed that you'd spring into Heaven. Why wouldn't you? If there's a God, perfect! Then you're there. You think He has something to do with this? You're dead wrong. He has nothing to do with this at all, nothing. He doesn't judge. He doesn't even judge you perfectly. You might have to judge Him perfectly just for a moment to get there but. . .

So here we sit at the end of time. Half of your minds are planning what you're going to do next week, and next year and tomorrow and you're all dead wrong. You're absolutely not real. You ready? This is not a real place. There's no such thing as place. Who knows about it? Trillions of stars all around you; all these things, and you reduce yourself to an oxygen-breathing nothing, and hold yourself so you can never get out of here. I watched what they had to do to get 150 miles in the air, because they are associated with the body. Cut it out! You can't even get to the closest star. You can go nowhere with your perceptual associations, and if that doesn't frustrate you, get out of here. The only reason I woke up is I couldn't stand the idea of not knowing what this was about. It's not religious. It hasn't got anything to do with hanging Jesus on the cross. It has nothing to do with that. It has to do with "What the hell is this all about?' Well it's all about everything and it's all about your own whole perfect mind. It has nothing to do with this. I hope that it has occurred to you that no one here knows the answer. Nobody knows where they came from or how they got here. Obviously. Is it time for you to wake up? Yeah. Really? "Am I really the savior?" Yes, you're really the savior. "What about the other guy?" What other guy? "Well, all these lovely brothers that I've constructed in my…" Phhhhhhhhhhttttttttt!!!

An idea cannot exceed its source, teacher. You keep struggling with your own concepts of forgiveness. They are absolutely meaningless. If sin is real, you're never going to forgive it. Never. You'll keep practicing until you discover you can't. But why take the long route? You see? This is the end of time. There's no proof of that. It requires your acceptance. That's why Jesus drew the circle and said, "I'm going to sit here until. . ." Can you understand this — that the alacrity of your mind, in determination to find this, is what salvation is? And that each moment you're making a decision to do this, and that's what salvation is, not your definition of the decision, you dummies. You keep making the decision and then trying to define where you are in association with it. You have no idea of the power of your own mind — None. None. Why? Mind is all power. You have no need of this. That's the great healing message, isn't it? Jesus said, "You need but say, 'I have no need of death and sickness,' and it will disappear." Can you do that with your patients? No, because you don't believe it, since you've created them to be sick to sustain your own self-identity. How the hell else would you serve here, if they didn't get sick? That's why you crucify the Christ. He's anti-establishment. He's anti-mortal. He's anti-death. He's anti-time. He's the opposite in all regards. Isn't he? You see?

So I stopped by to tell you there's a whole other association that you can enter into, and it will be all exactly the same as it looks here except it will be real bright and beautiful. OK? And it will be just a moment, and then you'll be out of time. It's called "The Rapture." It's taught in the Revelation as "The Rapture." We are entering "The Rapture." The world ends in 2006. This whole thing. . . Most of you won't last that long. Isn't that funny? This is going to be all over.

So, give up your grievances now. OK? Don't hold your resentments against the guy out there. He didn't do anything to you, did he? You did it. He's doing to you exactly what you think you did to him. Do you like that sentence from the *Course* or does that offend you? That's a nice sentence. You are the cause of your own pain. Most of you guys can't get the *Course* because you didn't really go through the psychological certainty that you're the cause of this. If you had had that. . . You may have to go through three or four more associations to see that you're doing this but to yourself. If you can see it now it will be a high advantage to you. You would stop holding a grievance against the other guy. Quit judging him. Quit finding him to blame. Don't find anybody to blame, ever again. Could you do that, find somebody NOT to blame, including yourself? You couldn't do that. You wouldn't be here. Somebody has to be responsible for this. Right? You have an authority problem. You'll accept responsibility for some of it, not all of it, so you project it in time and hold other associations. Boy, is that crazy! So time is going to be over now. And you'll be gone, and there is no world. You're not on a little mud ball, spinning at a thousand miles an hour, going around another. . . Look at! Here you are, standing right here, while all this stuff is going on around you. Do you see the illusion of the perceptual association? Why don't you fall off the earth? Why aren't you just spinning? You're holding it together in your own association in time. It'll just fade away. How does the earth disappear? It's just gone. It goes where it started. It's nowhere. Is there an Armageddon? That's nonsense, or one that you would make, yourself.

Many of you look very lovely, and if you see, many of these consciousnesses now are undergoing full revelation. They will give you the vision of your awakening if you'll allow them to. We're teaching vision to revelation or revelation to vision. Cause and effect are not apart. I cannot, obviously, show you my revelation, my whole mind. But I can show you our visional associations with each other if you'll allow me to. I have no reason to tell you this unless it's the Truth. I know you think I do, because you think I would benefit some way by our false association. You are dead wrong. You have a very strange value system.

It depends on death. And all of your associations depend on the exchange of scarcity. Exchange is impossible. You are under no laws but God's.

You guys come tomorrow morning and do Lesson 131, 132, and 76, and 139, and lessons 1 through 365! 131 and 132, 139. . . How do you miss 135? 76 — that's the most objectionable lesson in the *Course*. That lesson is not acceptable under any circumstances: Think further, you believe in the laws of companionship. They're all absurd. They're all crazy, and they're all nuts. They only share death. Don't do that anymore. You know really all you have to do? Just let the *Course* be true. Notwithstanding that it is true. The requirement is that you let it be true. Stop studying the source. You've got these weirdoes out there, that are studying the cause of the *Course In Miracles*, as though it could be anything but their own perceptual mind. It's just crazy. There's a lovely sentence in the *Course*. Jesus says that your whole problem — illusion — stems from the idea of the separation of cause and result. OK? Do you understand what I'm saying? The *Course In Miracles* is Jesus Christ. You are your own thoughts. They're not separate. This is the whole teaching of the *Course*. You don't have thoughts. You are the thoughts. [You say], "Well, let's study the associations of the historic Jesus with what he says in the *Course*." What the hell sense is there in that? They are not separate. The requirement is this: accept me or accept the effects. Both will work. Won't they? Do you understand that? With your heart, accept the teachings as whole. With your mind, accept the teachings as they are presented to you. Accept the cause or the effect. Jesus says, "If you can't believe me, believe what I tell you." Are they the same thing? Of course. But they are not the same thing in your mind because your mind is split in concepts. So you separate the cause and the effect. Everything in between is your own judgment. And that's what the falsity is.

See how easy that is? Now you can create. Why? You don't have to study your relationships of thought. This is the energy that you're seeing here. It's a re-association. This is the miracle of the *Course In Miracles*; of the thought-form associations that literally begin to create from the karma identity. You call this anything you want but these are. . . I'm just having thoughts. Thoughts are energy. Listen: all the Universe is, is thought. OK? God is only thought. God is only your idea. The problem is not that, the problem is: How much creative certainty is in your idea of God? For crying out loud! If you hold it in a limited thought-form, there's no energy. Don't you see? There's no extension from it. It just holds itself. It's such a narrow range. It doesn't have a broad range of color in it. It's real thin. Now, what happens to you as you broaden this association of the Great Rays is the thought that you had last week now has broadened into a new connective association. What do you do? You begin to create with your thoughts. I want you guys to create. For goodness sake! Can you actually change your identity through the creation assertion of yourself? Of course. I don't know what you think you are. Everybody that comes around me likes [this creative energy] I mean they all go out [and do really well]. Everybody does really well. If you're satisfied with that, that's fine with me. Actually I am offering you a whole mind. If you're not fearful of me, you'll discover that you'll create better, you'll paint, you'll dance, you'll do all sorts of things. Everybody has experienced that. If you become satisfied with that, and want to stay there and die, obviously, that's a decision that you're making. But I am telling you now that this portal is open. I'm giving you a fact. And all you will have to do to come into this association is say, "That's what I'm going to do." The second that you said that, you would open up the text of *A Course In Miracles*, and you would see it entirely differently. You've made the decision to see what it says. Now you're blinding yourself from the fear of seeing what it says. Got it? Eternity shouldn't threaten you guys. OK?

How come you teach physical awakening? The most difficult thing you'll have with the *Course In Miracles* or any teachings of physical resurrection, is the resurrection is physical. Do you understand me? That each moment, you are reconstructing yourself wholly in a physical body that must undergo the resurrection. That is literally true. And that's fearful to you. And the demonstrations of it are fearful. You see? Some of you don't particularly like demonstrations of mind coming free. Is it necessary that you do that? It has nothing to do with phenomena. It's necessary that you don't judge it except in your determination to undergo the inevitable process that you're experiencing. If I can just simply get you to say, "I am undergoing a transformation." All right? "I have nothing to do with it." OK? I am teaching now very simply, "I have no choice in the matter; it is going to occur. It is a natural metamorphosis; an evolutionary process of return. I will not judge it. I will let it happen." And if you'll come and be in this energy, it will happen to you very rapidly. Why? You don't bring your own judgments into it. It's the same idea as letting go and letting God. I'm sure you know that. OK? Don't judge it, in other words. There's another way to look at it. But it's important now that you see that this re-association of thought-forms is real. It's a real new dream happening to you. Otherwise you'll just die. You'll hold it from you; you'll keep studying it perceptually; you'll laud the teachers and call them the "father of the *Course*." That's the biggest crap I have ever heard! See? You'll go to the scribe, and give value to the thought-form association. That's absolutely meaningless. It has nothing to do with the *Course In Miracles*. This is only the transformation of your mind. OK? Now, this segment of time, in your own memories, has been blocked off for you. This is what the *Course* says; I'll do it like the *Course* says, it's literally been blocked off for you. If you will work the miracle, I'll adjust the time. I promise you that I'll adjust time for you, if you will let the miracle happen, and not be afraid. Why? The whole re-association will occur, because this portal is open later in time. I know you are fearful to do it because it will cause you to have to look at the conflict you've previously been in, in your association.

You will relinquish your self-identity. Because you did. OK? So now, actually, literally, there is a new reflection going on here, that you can sense and feel and glorify in, if you take all of your previous grievances, and forgive them and come into this new association. Just for a minute, lay aside your opinions and your judgements about what salvation ought to be, and come on home; because I guarantee you that it is your necessity to know what it ought to be, is what's keeping you from being it. You understand? Don't tell God about Himself. He already knows Who He is.

These are your light associations. You can get out of your judgements now, a little bit. You're bringing your time together. Some of you are very familiar to me. He's your Savior. OK! What's occurring to you now is you're losing the beam in your eye here and you're opening up your pineal, the ajna. See that? This is a physical occurrence. I don't want you to think [it's not physical]. I don't want to put a lot of emphasis on the glandular association, but I assure you that you have activated your pituitary associations in your ductless glands. That's happening. You have a tendency to put a little emphasis on it, and try to study the Churches of The Revelation with the chakras. That has nothing to do with it. But it is a physical undertaking, and you should begin to experience this. A new association of the projections of your own mind. That's what whole mind is, for goodness sake! Remember that when you look at it dualistically, you are giving it objective reality. "Know ye not you [must be born again]?" "If your eye offends you pluck it out." All of the statements of Jesus Christ from two thousand years ago were directly what I'm telling you now. Right? Never mind the splinter in your brother's eye. Look at the beam in your eye. You have to be one-eyed. Come together in that association. That's what's happening to you. You will, as he says, see things anew. The higher step to that, in the *Course*, is, these are just your projections and they will change according to the change of your mind. Literally change. Not change so that one thing gets a little better, and another gets a little worse. I mean, the whole thing changes in the manner in which you're seeing. Literally. It's as though all conceptions are going on all the time, and you can see them in any association that you have with yourself. That's literally true. That's why I want you to come now to a later time-frame where you can experience the harmony of your own thought-forms. Remember, you are only in conflict with your own thoughts, guys. And if you will start to create from this new you, later on in time, you will discover the harmony of that re-association. You see that? You see this? Some of you might like to know that we are all out of time together. I have to tell you this. This is the way Jesus teaches and it's a nice way to teach it. Obviously, we are nothing but one final memory together, and if you attempt to construct it, as we do in the *Course*, then we are actually out of time together, and have come back into this association. We are literally recollecting ourselves. That's what saviorship is. You're a deep seed of your own memories, aren't you? You see? Now you are waking up to the certainty and you're taking [responsibility]. Your burden is very light. Isn't it? You continue to bring the burden of your own memories into this re-association. That's why you're the savior of the world. You see this?

Some of you new guys look bright. You come tomorrow. I'll do this tomorrow. Some of you have got problems. I'll take care of your problems. I won't let you die. We need all the help we can get. Once you enter into this, if you were going to have an experience, we don't allow [you to leave the body]. We don't want you to do that. I want you in this body. Do you understand that? I don't need you in some other association. Why? What's wrong with the one you've got? You keep thinking somehow in the future, you can have a better association. That's not possible. It's impossible to get this too soon. You're always tempted when you get close, to say, "Well, I'm not quite ready. I've got to go through another death." Stop it! Stop adjusting. Just as you are, I want you. Don't change it. Don't change any of it. Stop trying to judge where you are in this association. You'll fit perfectly. Do you see it? How could you not fit? Wow! You see, we need to hold you in that, though. I want you in this body. We'll do the repairs. Look at this one. It works good. You're out of time. Look at this. Feel this? A hundred and twenty-two years. In this association? Yes. It's working all right, see? I'm integrating it. See? I hold you together in this association. Now obviously nothing is going to happen to it. You could prove me wrong, I suppose, by taking a dagger and stabbing me to death — couldn't you? — which is what you'll do. But it will have absolutely no effect on this association. Why? You've already done that with the thought of it. Do you hear me? Some of you really can hear me. OK? This is the whole teaching. Every time you think of that assassination, it's occurring. Everything is occurring. But what are we going to do? We're going to come together in this new harmony, and hold this association. That's true holy relationship. It has no judgement in it at all. All it is, is a single declaration for out-of-timeness. That's what a holy relationship is. It has nothing to do with this relationship. Nothing. How would it not be holy? It's your own whole mind. It's not a comparison of holiness. It's not any kind of comparison at all. It's love.

How would you not love a single goal? A single goal is what I'm teaching. Non judgment. Single goal. And this is my assignment. That might help you to hear that. I guarantee you this is my assignment. Or why do you think I'm here? Who do you think got you into this stuff? Me. Of course. I would have to, otherwise I couldn't get you out. But I can get you out. Why? I got you in. See the admission of the mistake, how important this is in your mind? It's imperative. One way in. One way out. Can I accept responsibility for it? Of course. It's not real. You don't know. If you did you would have to see it's not real because you couldn't stand the burden. For just that moment in time, the perfect altar place is where the defiled part of you lies. This is the way the *Course* teaches it. That's true. That's the whole idea of the schism, and it lies there, just together. And that's this horrifying moment that many of you have experienced in your Gethsemane. Haven't you? Now you pass through that veil, then you're in the borderland, and the bright light is all around you. Now, for that moment you're very valuable to us. Why? All of the memories that you have come rushing to that association. Sure. Oh yeah, that's the fun part. They are only constructions of your mind. That's why the whole basis of it is that you accept Atonement for yourself. That's the requirement.

There's a lot of healing going on here. These are light beings. There's no such thing as sickness. Just cut it out. This is what Jesus calls resurrection. In the Eastern thing it is known as the crown opening. It's very rare in this association, but it's obviously occurring. The opening of the crown is just the parting of the veil. If you look at your microcosm as a macrocosm you would see that the resurrection occurs only in this association. So you would see that, at any moment, this is what the resurrection is. We will do some body demonstrations tomorrow. I'll show you the difference in a phantom body and a body that's coming whole — that has become a hologram. Whereas this consciousness... How flat is this consciousness! You see, it has a little problem right there. But you want to be whole, don't you, with that association of you? That's nice. If you will stay out of perception with this energy, it will facilitate much more rapidly because you will admit to the process. That must be brought about by experience, and obviously the whole *Course* is nothing but teaching to the experience. The only thing that could possibly be shared is the experience. Obviously the concepts can't be shared. That's the whole teaching of the *Course*. Since you have restricted, in your perceptual association, the wholeness of you, the relinquishment of that is what the miracle is, and that's what's happening. OK! Nice.

So here we are at the end of time. There's no such thing as tomorrow. You've laid your yesterdays aside; for just a moment, you're going to say, "Father into Thy hands I commend my spirit," instead of saying, "Why have you forsaken me?" — and all the other junk that you said up until this time. And you'll be able to step out. That's very lovely. I think we'll have a quiet time. You guys want to have a little meditation? Be real gentle. I'll tell you why: the veil is open and some of you may spring out. That's all perfectly OK. There's no reason why you shouldn't. Look at this for a minute. Some of you are giving this a real pattern of reality. That's very nice. See that? That's a nice association. This is what, then? A field of dreams, isn't it. That sounds like a song cue. Gently now. Be real gentle with this for a moment because... You see... I am not getting a lot of resistance.

Discourse with Master Teacher

An Invitation

Enter in this new perspective
Where you're already resurrected

A Joyful Realization

Into the conflict I go
Merely to say it's not so

Nancy Reid

I Remember…

Dear Beloved,
I can only express my deepest love and gratitude.
You called and I remembered…
Thank you for the Truth, Beauty, Glory and Grace of You.

The stirring of my remembrance of our meeting at the No-Regrets Café came to me as an internal alarm clock going off, signaling me of an appointment made long ago. Yet, I could not remember what the appointment was, but only that I had to keep it, and I felt that I did not have much time or I would miss it. It was as if I were blind, desperately groping around trying to locate the invitation card, hoping that when I finally did lay my hands on it, I would remember. But I never found it; and, time was running out... Then, by grace, it found me instead. It was like a *Deus ex machina* — it showed up as an encounter with the Master Teacher, and in a fraction of a second, I was re-oriented, and I actually saw that it was a meeting with my Self.

Right now, this moment, we are meeting at the Café, reminiscing about our excursion into this place and time, viewing it through the holograph that you know of as "your life." You may have not remembered that all the characters, including the one you call yourself, and everything happening to you and in your world is part of your story, but the fact remains that it is your story and that you are the one telling it. We are always meeting each other and indeed, always meeting our Self. It could not be otherwise: there is only one Self. How could there be regrets or grievances, except in the forgetting the nature of everything? Miracles are messages sent from your Self reminding you that you are the storyteller and that there is another story — a story of love and forgiveness — that you can tell.

Let us remember this story of the forgiven world:

> *Can you imagine how beautiful those you forgive will look to you? In no fantasy have you ever seen anything so lovely. Nothing you see here, sleeping or waking, comes near to such loveliness. And nothing will you value like unto this, nor hold so dear. Nothing that you*

remember that made your heart sing with joy has ever brought you even a little part of the happiness this sight will bring you. For you will see the Son of God. You will behold the beauty the Holy Spirit loves to look upon, and which He thanks the Father for. He was created to see this for you, until you learned to see it for yourself. And all His teaching leads to seeing it and giving thanks with Him.

This loveliness is not a fantasy. It is the real world, bright and clean and new, with everything sparkling under the open sun. Nothing is hidden here, for everything has been forgiven and there are no fantasies to hide the truth. The bridge between that world and this is so little and so easy to cross, that you could not believe it is the meeting place of worlds so different. Yet this little bridge is the strongest thing that touches on this world at all. This little step, so small it has escaped your notice, is a stride through time into eternity, beyond all ugliness into beauty that will enchant you, and will never cease to cause you wonderment at its perfection.

This step, the smallest ever taken, is still the greatest accomplishment of all in God's plan of Atonement. All else is learned, but this is given, complete and wholly perfect. No one but Him Who planned salvation could complete it thus. The real world, in its loveliness, you learn to reach. Fantasies are all undone, and no one and nothing remain still bound by them, and by your own forgiveness you are free to see. Yet what you see is only what you made, with the blessing of your forgiveness on it. And with this final blessing of God's Son upon himself, the real perception, born of the new perspective he has learned, has served its purpose.

The stars will disappear in light, and the sun that opened up the world to beauty will vanish. Perception will be meaningless when it has been perfected, for everything that has been used for learning will have no function. Nothing will ever change; no shifts nor shadings, no differences, no variations that made perception possible will still occur. The perception of the real world will be so short that you will barely have time to thank God for it. For God will take the last step swiftly, when you have reached the real world and have been made ready for Him.

The real world is attained simply by the complete forgiveness of the old, the world you see without forgiveness. The Great Transformer of perception will undertake with you the careful searching of the mind that made this world, and uncover to you the seeming reasons for your making it. In the light of the real reason that He brings, as you follow Him, He will show you that there is no reason here at all. Each spot His reason touches grows alive with beauty, and what seemed ugly in the darkness of your lack of reason is suddenly released to loveliness. Not even what the Son of God made in insanity could be without a hidden spark of beauty that gentleness could release.

All this beauty will rise to bless your sight as you look upon the world with forgiving eyes. For forgiveness literally transforms vision, and lets you see the real world reaching quietly and gently across chaos, removing all illusions that had twisted your perception and fixed it on the past. The smallest leaf becomes a thing of wonder, and a blade of grass a sign of God's perfection.

From the forgiven world the Son of God is lifted easily into his home. And there he knows that he has always rested there in peace. Even salvation will become a dream, and vanish from his mind. For salvation is the end of dreams, and with the closing of the dream will have no meaning. Who, awake in Heaven, could dream that there could ever be need of salvation? —

Jesus Christ (*A Course In Miracles*, Chapter 17)

I love you. Welcome Home!

Clare Lamanna

Friends

Gladly with you I'll chance,
Clasping hands we go...
In this honest grasp our truth relayed;
A gleaming glance, a knowing nod,
And a powering pact is forged.
What seemed never to come is here now,
A present force, an energy ushered in,
Our direction now conjoined in One.
The innocent venture now a quest,
In revolution we ride.
We the regents and princes,
Agents of advance, envoys of infinity,
Comrades of universal birthright, true allies and cohorts,
Accomplices in a great escape.
This adventure of friends leaves none alone,
Or bound in the sleep of time,
For gathering in is the bond of these brothers,
A contract of honor and privilege, gratefully enacted;
An unlimited alliance of two, uniting all.
To you dear companion I remain in debt,
For a heart unlocked, a spirit recalled, and an odyssey begun.
A due carried with unending thanks,
Its claim to be eagerly met.

John G.

The Universe Maria Wereżyńska

Oh, Brother, where art thou? At the No-Regrets Café.

The Atonement is a corporate venture, and at the No Regrets Café everyone is welcome. There are no dark spots in the mind, the Son is shining, and no one is still without a Café Latte or an Espresso. My best intentions were not helpful at all; what brought me here was the grace of God, and a little willingness.

Father, into Thy Hands I commend my Spirit in its entirety. I love You, with all my heart, with all my soul and strength, and with all my mind, and my brother as myself.

Light shines, and only shines. Light is simply, totally ignorant of darkness. Jesus is my saviour, Jesus is the Light that I am. I am what you are. And here we come together, at the funeral of the second person (you) and third person (s/he), and the singular fulfillment of the first pluralistic we. Oh, the joy at the end of time!

What a fine frequency we enjoy together. Celebrations usually begin and end with a hot beverage. God is in a hot beverage. Let's see who is ready to dissolve into the formless. I certainly am. Just one more line, before the joy becomes indescribable. God must be the mind with which we think. Who else delivers mind? Gosh, I wish all of us came together like this. In holiness things look very lovely. Is it Christmas already?

Give my Love to everyone, I am not gone when I leave, robed with roses and a smile. Who else than you could it be? The universe has one Lover and it is you. The stars knew it all the way through. What a fine mind you are, your Father is very proud of you. See our friend over there? He doesn't have any regrets at all.

And now, I must excuse myself. It has been a total pleasure to leave the meaningless behind with you. I'll see you on the other side, in just an instant. As someone used to say — and here we are, and here we are, together, right here and right now. At the No Regrets Café. I love you. God bless us all.

Andreas Pröhl

A Cup of Coffee

So this is it?

Yeah.

There's nothing else then?

No. Do you have any questions?

No, not really. It is just so effortless and so simple.

Yeah, you think it's impossible, too difficult, too hard, until you see it, understand it, look through it.

Yeah. And then it doesn't make sense that this could ever not have been.

Amazing.

Yeah. Isn't that so?

Uh-hmm.

Miriam Menting

The Joy of Instantaneous Communication

*In the beginning was the Word,
and the Word was with God, and the Word was God.*

A Course In Miracles tells you that you can hear God's Voice no matter where you are and no matter what you are doing. He is always available to you. This goes beyond the idea of prayer in a church, beyond any idea of a struggle to reach God. He is here with you and you can hear Him effortlessly. There is a part of your mind that is in communication with its Creator every instant, right now. You are in direct communication with God in the recognition that you are as God created you. It is not about the words you use, but it is about what you are trying to express. The intent. Prayer is communication. But always in the awareness of what it is you are asking for.

This moment offers you a direct experience of God, and the words are only the means to an end. In this world everything relies on words, vocabulary, trying to express the right things in the right way. Communication, whole and perfect, goes beyond this world altogether. It is instantaneous, and it has nothing to do with words that are spoken. Now you are open to the moment, now you listen and are alert, now you ask for the experience to be shown the way, to know the truth.

It is really that simple, and that immediate. You invite God and He answers. It might seem to take a moment, in that moment the silence is deafening and you might get lost in the idea that you weren't heard and that it failed, and then suddenly the answer dawns on you, suddenly God is here, and in that moment all time disappears and you know with certainty that you are one with Him.

All you have to do today is listen to God's healing Voice. Today is the day where you will seek, hear, learn and understand, because this day has been chosen. There is no need to focus on the world and its chaos, simply call on God and listen. Prayer is active communication with God that goes on every single moment. You experience that you are not a body, you are free. Your home awaits you. And you make the declaration that it is all you want. If you so choose, you can depart this world entirely, simply through a change of mind about the purpose of the world. It now has the purpose of awakening to truth, of remembering who you are.

This world was over long ago. The only reason you are seeing it, in this moment, is because you want to. And every action of your mind is directed toward making this world true for you. It's not true. It doesn't exist. As you apply the workbook lessons, as you think about the lesson for the day and let related thoughts come to you, you start to feel something that has nothing to do with any specifics. It is a quiet recognition, a sense of peace, of love, of eternity. This is Who you really are. This is communication with God. Let it be through the Holy Spirit, let it be through Jesus; you recognize this communication because it is what Heaven is. Heaven is right here and right now. It is not a place, not a condition, but a state of perfect peace.

So what are you waiting for? You are the one. All are called, but few choose to listen. Let it be you who listens today. The Word of God is unspoken and yet clearly heard. This is the time of your awakening.

Father, I come to You today to seek the peace that You alone can give. I come in silence. In the quiet of my heart, the deep recesses of my mind, I wait and listen for Your Voice. My Father, speak to me today. I come to hear Your Voice in silence and in certainty and love, sure You will hear my call and answer me.

Now do we wait in quiet. God is here, because we wait together. I am sure that He will speak to you, and you will hear. Accept my confidence, for it is yours. Our minds are joined. We wait with one intent; to hear our Father's answer to our call, to let our thoughts be still and find His peace, to hear Him speak to us of what we are, and to reveal Himself unto His Son.

Tanja van Steijn-Seely

Before Time Was Altma Medina

The Enigma of Faith:

You Don't Have Faith - You Give It

There is always an anomaly: The unusual occurrence that testifies to a new way of seeing. Today, the headlines arrested our attention with the story of the Amish community whose children had just been brutally murdered, sending a delegation to the family of the murderer to offer them the gift of forgiveness. Interviewed by an incredulous reporter, the Amish spokesperson was asked, "How can forgiveness be possible under such horrific circumstances?" From the grace of her own discovery, she expressed the experience of release available through the handing over of our anguish and vengeance to the healing mind of Christ. She spoke poignantly not of a religious doctrine but from the trust born of her own personal transformation. She witnessed to the change that occurs when we, individually, allow ourselves to be forgiven by a Mind whose forgiveness is total. It is this healing that is then increased through its extension. As Jesus expresses it in the *Course*, "It is the privilege of the forgiven to forgive."

Faith is not a static condition, or an accumulation of correct doctrinal references, but an active investment of trust in a thought system that belies the thinking of the world. Is faith necessary? Absolutely. As we progress in the complete alteration of the definition we have about our self — in this process we call transformation, or illumination, or resurrection — our first miracle may occur accidentally, when we trust blindly, out of a desperate attempt to seek absolution for our pain or as "a last resort." In our necessity for an alternative to our perceived experience of suffering, it is a real "giving," past the conflictual appearance testified to by our perception.

Imagine the surprise, the gratitude, when we discover a new Reality, a Truth about our Self that testifies only to Love, Love that is unconditional, Love that is all-encompassing. As our "Holy Instants" of healing occur, that blind faith evolves into a certainty of a reference that is "not of this world. " As an action of the mind, faith constitutes a fundamental undoing, both of my emotional and my physical justification of my self. Yet, like our Amish friend, it requires a constant application. When accompanied by gratitude, faith develops into a realization of an inevitable process of species evolution that was witnessed to by Jesus in his resurrection.

Glad Hancock

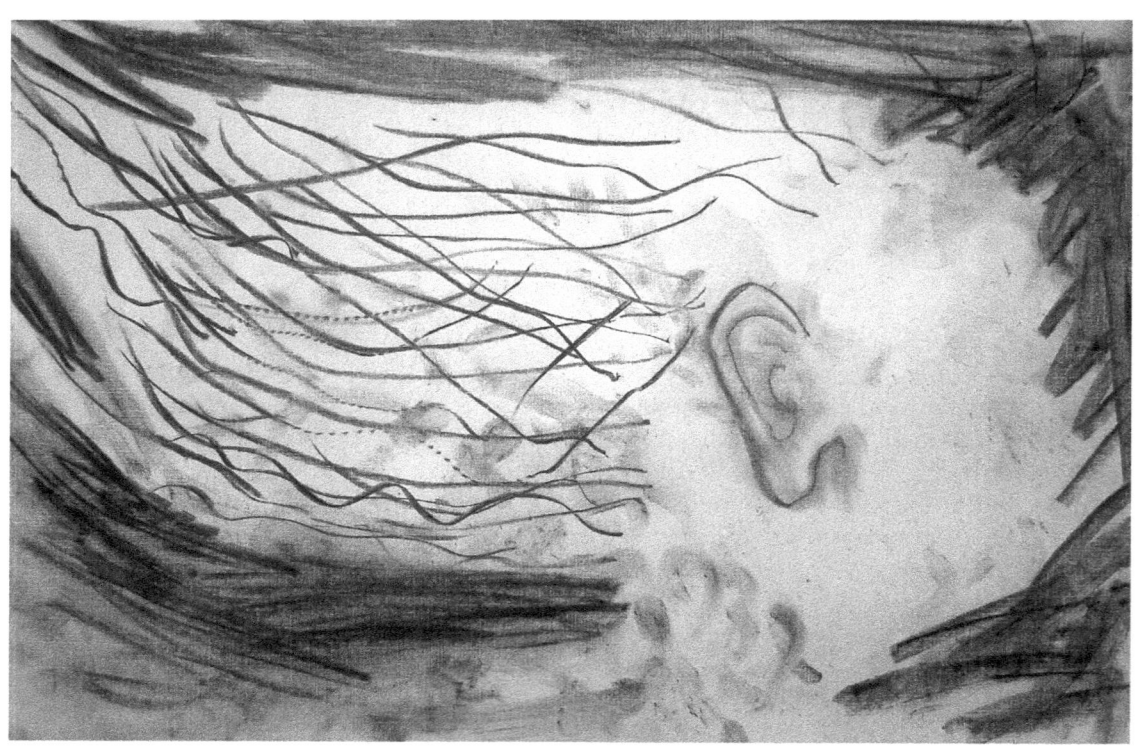

Ute Ringel

Someone Who Hears Me

Hey! Ever felt
the touch of an unseen hand,
gentle brushstrokes
against a bruised ego,
compassion extended
sudden as waking,
and the other so still, such intense listening,
our minds shift completely,
defenses collapsed,
the picture wholly changed.
The day shivers, ecstatic,
and splits wide open.

Pamela Schueller

We Meet In A Figure Of Your Reappearance

If you have come here during your visit to this café of no regrets, allow me, if you are willing to sit down with us for a moment and have a sip of our 'No-Regrets Chocolate Coke,' to relay to you two other demonstrations offered to us by the Master Teacher of what is occurring in our encounter here and what it represents in the truth of it.

Read carefully and notice we are offering you a miraculous entrance into a new idea of a space and a time, a clip of a continuum, in an appearance as a 'new figure,' as the 'resurrection of your body identity' and your inadvertent 'appearance as the Christ' or the wholeness of yourself:

> *What I am going to do with you, based on all of your old experiences, which you have projected into the future, is take a sequence of time (here is what a miracle is that you have now performed with me) in which you had intended to remain within this frequency of space for the entire forty thousand years, and had separated, [and turn it] into a moment where you no longer have to live within your identity. What are we actually doing? This is in the allowance for an appearance of a new figure of you that just a moment ago wasn't present in your association.*
>
> *This is the whole religious idea that you can be born again in the idea of the resurrection of your body identity. This is our whole teaching. There isn't anything that you haven't heard plenty of times. It's nothing that you have not identified when people suddenly appeared out of nowhere — what do you call them? The Christ Mind, or the idea of a variation? — only to find yourself reduced within the idea that the reflection of your light that you thought was going to save you turns out to just be a reflection of you.*
>
> *What I have done for you, if you'd like to really know within the*

sequence of the idea of dark form, is taken a clip of the idea of space-time. This is what we call the reappearance of a single whole mind of consciousness. This is the idea of teaching since we teach all the time, don't we? Are we teachers? Oh sure. We are teachers of the idea of where we seem to be located in quantum ideas of space-time that represent distances between ourself and ourself.

The idea that I am going to shorten that distance so that the reappearance of you can occur now, is what you were afraid was going to happen, and by rejecting the idea of the happening it doesn't happen. There is absolutely nothing new about this. The idea that I am getting a reflection of who I want to see within my continuum is the idea that you and I have recognized each other within a frequency of past and future association. I have taken the idea, in this new continuum of mind, and shortened the idea of past and future ideas to the idea of a present location. The idea that the brother, the idea that the guy that I saw out there, that I was fearful of identifying with, except in a limited idea, is simply the admission that I am going to let everybody cave in on me. And that's why I have been afraid. What I have discovered is, I have repeated sequences of time — what you call 'death' — within my mind so often that obviously there appears to be no idea of an alternative contained within my own mind. Why is that true? There is no identity!

And here is another Master Teacher demonstration of the wholeness of our encounter here, where death, and getting old and sick, are altogether taken out of the equation of what we share as we are sitting together and enjoying each other's company in the love that we feel at this very instant:

It's impossible that in the reference we are sharing of our mind, you can actually be sick, or get old, or die. Why? You have acknowledged responsibility for the act of separation. Turn and look at the guy right next to you. I'm curious to see... Here's a guy next to you that is a reflection of your own mind that you have condemned to body formulation based on your own formulation. Now I'm sitting next to you. There! Did you turn and look at him? Did, just for a second, you begin to recognize each other in the power of your mind, through forgiveness, to love one another? Here is the power of love that I am offering you: there is nothing to be afraid of. Don't be afraid. I am leading you in your body re-identification to a point where you are going to collapse your body. What does it have to do with death? Don't be silly! You are already dead! Death is an idea that has taken form in your mind and constitutes the emotional involvement you have of suffering and loss and pain, and the idea that the things that you love are going to leave you. And the ordeal of suffering that you are undergoing is nothing but your identification of yourself as a body.

There are some spiritual seekers and searchers who like the idea of spirit being its entirety and attempt to dis-associate themselves from the body. It won't work. The constitution of the idea that you are a body, which you are, must be converted in its entirety, utilizing the idea of the power of light and love. It's called physical resurrection. What does it have to do with coming here, and dying, and getting old and believing that you're a body? Nothing. I'm in your dream of death, interrupting your cycle of repetition of self, out in the universe, in a billion years, that — we use the term 'gravity' — have curved you back, and you're ending up exactly where you started. The speeding up of the idea of re-location can occur immediately in your mind if you decide for a moment to locate yourself where the source and entirety of your problem is. This is a point in space-time within your galactic association that you were previously fearful of coming to.

But now you are here. Welcome home! Have a snack.

Wolter van Verschuer

He is In Everything I See Maria Wereżyńska

Good News!

This just in from Jesus:

You are whole and perfect as God created you.
The world you see is of your own making and does not exist.
You are home in Heaven where you have never left.

Ah_____ What a relief!

Elaine Miller

The No-Regrets Café

Sitting on a stool at the bar of the No-Regrets Café, I look at all the faces expressing themselves, laughing, whispering secrets, telling stories, and then being replaced by other faces laughing, whispering secrets, telling stories, creating the mosaic of faces, unworldly encounters all blending one into another, being one thing. Time comes and goes, faces change, timelessness is the only constancy.

Reflecting on the first time I encountered the No-Regrets Café, I remember that it was a warm, overcast fall day. I walked through the doors, my arms full, carrying artwork to display for an event in Revelation Hall and there it was, just to the left of the entrance, the No-Regrets Café, shining like a beacon in a storm. I was drawn to it immediately. The gleaming white bar in a complete, perfect circle, no break in its continuity; it stood as an altar. I was struck with an overwhelming sense of happiness and gratitude for all who put their love and energy into creating such a special place for me, a portal for meeting out of time.

This perfect circle, this symbol of wholeness, reminded me of my wedding ceremony; all the guests stood around us forming a circle signifying the boundless circle of love, no beginning, no end.

This place of no regrets is a meeting place out of time and space. It is where legions gather to marvel in the light; it is like little children on the playground laughing, insouciant, playing in joyful innocence. This is the playground of light where we gather to remember the truth of who we are, recognizing our innocence, and we, too, play insouciantly, with no regrets.

Christine Slack Comeau

Ute Ringel

Ever Present Treasure

Today the day has finally come at last
I just arrived and now there is no past
For here all that is true stands whole and clear
And in my mind there is no conflict dear

So let us rise to join and seize the day
And celebrate this final passion play
For this the day that is God's Gift to me
And in my joy are all of you made free

His Peace reigns full with more and more to give
And in His Holy Light my Self does Live
So please forgive my daft and foolish game
For thinking you and I were not the same

By Grace the Truth has dawned on eyes that see
And now my heart is full of Love that's free
The Fountain springs again from desert sands
And all we are is safe within God's Hands

The circle now expands and opens wide
Revealing Heaven's Treasure that's inside

Kristen Lynn Kloostra

A New Way

It comes as a slipping,
A draw, like a gentle tide.
When at first, ankle deep, a playful welcome;
Now enveloped, this ocean's might revealed.
Only an instant stands for retreat,
The familiar shore beckons...
I will not turn back.
The drudgery of that known land
will not sway this mate again.
Carry me, strange new swell,
An untold voyage do I crave.
Of mishap and blessing,
calamity and fortune.
A new way, in any case.

John G.

"Regrets?" ...Only Light

God is the Light in which I see.
    Full.
    Pervasive.

   God is my Father. This Light is my Source.

I and my Father are One.
   I am that Light.

   I am.

Beautiful. Radiant. All-inclusive.
   Nothing waits outside of Me.
      No one, nothing, awaits healing.

In light is only purity. Grace. Everything simply perfect, now
   and forever.

My burden is ever only this light.

Light is never heavy.
   This light is not dark.
      It is not morose.

Only free. Full of love. Naked. Clear.

   Pure.

In light is understanding. Truth.
   Everything is ever forgiven. Kindness smiles, caresses all its
children unceasingly in this light. All hearts are opened.

God's holiness is here. My holiness. Yours.

'Regrets? '... finally, a word unknown.

   But love is known. Our beautiful light.
Shared in holiness. Forever.

                                         Karyn Aldin

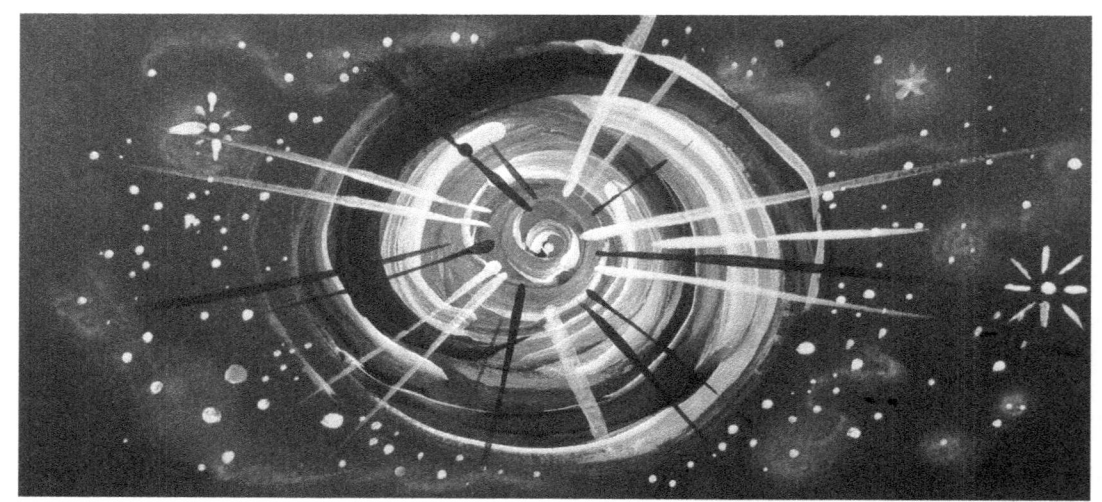

Origin Maria Wereżyńska

Brightstar Lane

Gliding down the bardos
Of dawn-drenched clouds
Bright stars showing the way,
I'm a little brought back
to where the beginning
is gone and the end
is just another way
to begin.

Where cause and effect meet
in the middle
and separation forgets
to appear while here and there
are one and the same
for yesterday
and tomorrow
are part of this now
making it easy to see
what all of it is.

I've been given away.

With the good-natured watcher
to share what is free
...to inwardly smile
at the centuries long seconds
who tick off the lessons
learning to listen
the way mountain is polished by sun
washed by the storm
kissed by the moon
its story sung by the wind
restored in the fire
and caressed by my stars,
I'm a little brought back
to where the beginning
is gone and the end
is just another way
to begin.

Wesley Buniger

Waves of Light

How could I know where a beam of light goes
Or see how the smallest atom flows
Why would I care how a flower grows
In the river of life — converting in the fire
beyond the forms of night — waves of endless light

I can be at the end of time
Reach to the furthest star
It was born in my mind
It is creation divine
You are all of what I am
The dream has come to an end
It was born in God's mind
It is created divine

How could I know where universes go
Space and time always moving slow
Why would I care — heaven still glows
Within the Peace of God — streams of endless love
Angels all in flight — eternity in sight

I don't know about relativity
Quantum theory is just a mystery
Without love it's just a misery
Into the Heart of God — within the realms of light
Everything is all right — leaving on the next flight

Eric Gatehouse

A Personal Awakening Experience

The only real true method of teaching in the initial encounter is the entire rejection of the conceptual association. Those of you who have been with me understand that fundamentally I have no interest in your erstwhile talents whatsoever. This is obviously Ramana Maharshi. My interest is only in you in the completion of your own process. That's just the way it is.

The necessity for that is very simply at the level of your heretofore consciousness association. You somewhere were in a presumption that there was value in the specific act of the creative purpose that you were using. It isn't that there was not value in it, but it would be almost impossible for you to express it in the fullness of your creative necessity without having it reflect to the gratification of your egotistical associations. I've never really tried to express that before, but I want you to see the evidence of it. Certainly if that energy procedure — let's use painting silk screen — certainly that well could end up in my association with you, at the minimum, cutting off your own ear. Are you familiar with that? Are you familiar with whopping off your own ear because you can't stand the limitation of your own creative mind? That was a physical happening of a very famous painter. The passion that I am offering you will be of such an intense nature that if I have directed you to a specific acknowledgment of your previous limitations, I would in effect be denying you the totality of your own mind. This is not open to discussion; this is a fact of the matter. This is what I do and what I am.

I have no real concern about what you bring me as to the nature of the manner in which you have become who you are in your relationship with me. It is not that it does not have value, but it only has value to the extent that you will admit that you are about to attempt to pursue a new course in which your own talents will be minimal, or progressively non-necessary for you. If you came to me, and I am speaking from my whole mind, and you said to me, "My name is so-and-so, I'm a doctor (or I'm a lawyer or I'm an Indian chief)." I am not concerned about it. My unconcern is what your salvation is. That's not true because I say it's true. It's true because I'm not concerned.

The truth of that matter is that I can't recognize human beings in their associations with themselves. I haven't been able to since my illumination. That is, I can operate on the premise that your name is so-and-so. I can be in the world and apparently participate with people with names, but I find no correspondence with them at all, and haven't since my illumination. It wouldn't mean anything to me. You could present me with any problem that you had, and while I would recognize it, I would not make an attempt to solve it within the association with you. That's just me.

How that came about is something because it came about. I'll use Wisconsin for a minute. I've never talked about this before. Obviously with what occurred to me, I had a full intention of being me, whatever I'm being right now. If I moved up, by some sort of miracle association, to a place in Wisconsin I call "God's Country Place," in no manner did I attempt to attract anyone. It didn't occur to me. I didn't know how to do it. If you would like an example of it, I have lived seven miles outside of a town called Reedsburg for ten years and I haven't spoken to anybody in ten years — it seems as though somewhere it never occurred to me — except to say hello. And this is a town that has seen little kids grow up and graduate, and I go in the same grocery store, and suddenly ten years has passed. And I'm not mayor of Reedsburg, which I would have been in about two years had I been my former self. So to me that seemed perfectly natural. It seems a little strange now because apparently I'm going to be able to say, "Hello." But in some manner I was accepted into the community. It isn't that people did not know that I lived out there, and I think the reason for it is that I didn't really pay any attention to them, so I was not a threat to them. There was no way that I became a threat, I simply lived there. That's the only way I can explain it. I drive a car that says, "Disabled Veteran." So they recognize me.

If you decide to go out and do this on your own, and you're going to cover your Christhood, you have to put up some sort of front association. This is just the way it will be. If I sent you on a mission here with a whole mind, I would expect you initially to garb yourself in a manner that would be acceptable initially in the attraction of the associations that were ready to hear you. That would be true whether you would be in Nazareth or wherever you would be.

The progression that has occurred in this has been expressed by an expanding willingness of the individual association who has been seeking the entirety of the solution to the problem. That's what I am offering. It would be very unlikely that, under any particular circumstance, this beautiful gentleman right here might care to listen to me tell him that there is no world, and that I am here to take him home with me, and that he is perfect as God created him. He wouldn't mind me telling him that I have a new way I would like to share my life with him. Or, I have a new way that I have discovered where you and I can go into business together. Or, I have a new church that I want to open up where we can attract attention. You would want to have me offer you a way in which you could continue to participate in your activities based on the direction that I would give you that would satisfy you in your own association with yourself. That's just the way it is. I don't do that. I don't know how to do it. My instructions to you are that this is not a real world, and you are going to get old and suffer pain and die unnecessarily. That's the fact of the matter. That's not open to a discussion as far as I'm concerned. Why would I open it to a discussion? I know the world isn't real. If you are happy to hear that, bless you. If you're not happy to hear that, bless you.

It could start out in a couple different ways. It could start out as a total rejection, in which case they won't hear me at all. I'm not threatening them with anything. The second thing will be, "How come this guy is so uncompromising?" You are accustomed in your own spiritual teaching to teach conceptually the possibility of some sort of illumination. The conceptual possibility of illumination is not what it is, and it is not what I teach. Your illumination as far as I'm concerned has nothing at all to do with your conceptual observation of it. If it did, you'd all be illuminate. You could be illuminate simply by judging yourself to be illuminate, which is the way most associations end up thinking they're illuminate.

The other factor involved in it is that it is impossible that I do not teach physical transformation because my transformation was physical. My transformation did not have to do with Christianity. It did not have to do with the doctrine of Zen. It did not have to do with the mystical horoscopes of the masters. My transformation was physical, because of the emergence in me of a solution that I found in a moment of revelation, that was explainable to me in my participation only under the new terms that I had found in that discovery. I really meant what I said, and I wish I could say it more simply than that.

You will have that initial experience, and this is called baptism, or the discovery of God, or an initial spiritual awakening. In my case, I was addicted to alcohol. I was addicted to everything. I was happily addicted to everything until I went into the hospital with cirrhosis of the liver. And I was still happily addicted to everything. So I couldn't solve the problem. I'm an example of a very successful problem-solver who isn't solving anything. That's the fact of the matter. I'm good at it. I was good at it since I was born. When that experience occurred with me, from then on all of my associations were based on a spiritual fact. Without explaining it to you, it was based on a spiritual fact that it happened to me and that it had entirely changed my life. I was relieved of an impossible association, one over which I had no control. (I'm talking about you, actually.) There was nothing I could do about it. Wherever I asked for help, or however that occurred, I'm not concerned about it. But from that moment on, I taught that there was a manner by which you could be relieved of any problem that you had simply by asking for help. How did I know that? I had had the experience.

I'll use the 12-Step Program for a minute, since I'm telling you how this worked for me. I discovered hundreds and thousands of other associations who had been in like conditions, who had undergone the same experience that I had. To me, that was astonishing! To me it was astonishing that I could go to a meeting. I'll use all of you guys: if all of us had come into this because we had overcome a single problem, we would immediately begin to share the overcoming of the problem rather than the problem itself. Have you got that? We would have in common — what? A spiritual experience that solved our problem. For those of you familiar with the 12-Step Program, this is exactly what the 12-Step Program is. Are you familiar with that? Who is familiar with Alcoholics Anonymous? Most of you have heard of the 12-Step Program. It is a spiritual program that says, "I am unmanageable. There is no way I can solve the problem. I'll make a decision to turn my will and my life over to God, and the problem will be solved."

But when I came together with associations, I discovered to my amazement that to one degree or another if they were happy in their new discovery it had come about because of a spiritual awakening. Do you hear me? Is there a question on this? The reason that I teach spiritual awakening — and if this is too degrading for you I'm sorry — is because I was awakened spiritually from a condition that was no longer tolerable. That is really all I teach here today. There is no doctrine in that particularly, except the simple doctrine of forgiveness, very simply because the resentments of my association were what was causing my addiction — that is, my pain and inability to deal with the identities.

The twelfth step of the Program, which is *A Course In Miracles,* is: "Having had a spiritual awakening as a result of these steps, I practice these principles in my affairs and carry the message to other addicts." That's what I do. What began to occur with me in my necessity of service, I was taught not to judge the value of the service that I was giving, but only to give it. Who taught me that? I knew that if I began to take too much associate credit for what was happening to me, they would base their credit on me for their sobriety — which was not true since I knew that my sobriety (or my enlightenment) came from God, not myself. It isn't that I intentionally did the right thing; I did the right thing very simply because I knew that I was not responsible for my condition. Is that so, Program people? So when somebody said to me, "Boy, you're really good at this, how long have you been on the Program?" I said I came on this morning. Can you hear that? My response to that would be, I'm sober today, just like I'm telling you — today is the only day. I matured with teaching "one day at a time," which is what I still teach. What happened is that this began to fit more and more into a way of life for me.

The other thing that impressed me about it is that I was able to function at a very high level in the world, with an underlying acknowledgment of a problem that we had solved in mutuality in the world, without the necessity to acknowledge it to the world. I organized and had private Alcoholics Anonymous meetings where people would come who needed to maintain their anonymity. Can you hear this? This has changed, I'm going back quite a while — 25 years. If a man was desperate, and found a solution through the Program, and had to retain the anonymity — I could meet in an association with a judge or with a doctor or with a lawyer or with a clergyman or with anyone — we would meet and do this association with each other, and we could meet out in the world and acknowledge each other without the necessity to acknowledge it to the world. It is a lovely thing. They could trust me, or we could trust each other, to acknowledge our unmanageability and the solution through God and still operate in the world.

In that sense, your unmanageability can be unacknowledged. But somewhere you are going to have to acknowledge it to God and yourself and perhaps one other person. That's the fifth step of the Program. Somewhere you are going to have to tell somebody about all your problems. Maybe you're going to have to write them out. This is the Workbook of the *Course*. Do you understand? In the process, I could go out in the world; I was in the real estate business, and all that sort of thing; but we would meet and it was as though we had a secret association. You know why? We did! I would no more think of breaking the anonymity — it would be the last thing I would do. I wouldn't dream of doing that. If he wanted to go to an open meeting and stand up and give a talk, that was fine with me. But there was no way that I was going to disclose to the world that he had found peace and happiness through the grace of God. It is not that it did not change his life, and reflect in what he did in the world, but the world would not have recognized the totality of his unmanageability. Did you hear that? The world would not have recognized that the doctor botched an operation and killed a patient. Anybody could confess to me with the certainty that his confession had to do with the contrition of the realization of his recovery, not his determination to perform the fraudulent nature in which he is.

I was able to look at the fallacies of people and forgive them from the certainty that we're all fallible, and that the abominations that are going on in this world are incredible, and that no one really confesses to the other guy how much of that there is out there. This was the growth of my personal experience.

The only other element that's involved in it was my necessity to carry the message. Since I am a communicator, it's what I do. I'm a communicator. I'm a television star. I know how to do that. I grew up doing that. That's what I am. When I discovered *this*, I never lost my necessity to communicate it. I needed to carry the message. Obviously this is not different than carrying the message of anything. But for me, fortunately, it was carrying the message of — what? My spiritual awakening! So it turned into a necessity for me to serve. In other words, if somebody called on the telephone and somebody made a desperation call, the answering service would know particular people to call; I would get a call, and I would go out. So I went out in service and met all sorts of different people in all sorts of different circumstances. Everything from the worst dark alley you could ever find at 2 o'clock in the morning, to a big mansion up on the hill, with a guy who had given his wife a black eye — whatever it was. I would come up and walk in and sit with the solution if they were willing to accept it. So that's what I did. And I did it along with operating a business and all of that sort of thing.

Somewhere in that process I observed more and more people having an experience that I could see happening to them. There were occasions when I would get, say, the president of Sears, a real high executive who was totally unmanageable — dear ones when I say totally unmanageable, I mean *totally* unmanageable — and no one knew it. If they knew it, they wouldn't even tell each other. Did you ever see a situation where the boss was so bad nobody even talks about it to themselves? It was like that. What a beautiful guy. And this is an example. I took him to Elgin. Elgin is our mental institution outside of Chicago. It's the worst place he could ever have been. And he came out of it the next morning, and he was sitting there in a chair with paper slippers and puke all over his bathrobe, and I'm sitting next to him there with my suit and tie, and he's just looking around. His situation... Folks, that's about as hopeless a situation as I have ever seen. He had gone from the mansion on the hill to suddenly sitting in this place with bars on the windows and blithering things around him, and here I am sitting next to him. And if you have ever shared a low point, those who have perhaps worked in this field and have had people experience low points, that point was about as low as anything that I have ever seen. That point was so low that it made the whole place low. It was just utter and total devastation, and I'm sitting right there with it. The difference was that I knew that in ten minutes I was going to get up and go out and get into my new Lincoln. I knew that I was out of it. So I was able to be in that situation — for all the reasons I can think of — including feeling the incredible compassion by my realization that I had been in the same boat that he was in. Do you hear me? What I'm really talking about is this: I had been in that boat, I had had that experience and I had had an experience that had overcome it.

I didn't counsel them. I never sympathized with people telling them they were drunk for all of the reasons. I never told them they were unmanageable because of their wife or their kids or their job. I told them they were unmanageable for one single reason, and that was ethyl alcohol. Just as I tell you you're unmanageable for one single reason: you are addicted to death — no other reason. You have one problem and I'm offering you one solution. I hadn't evolved that, but that's what it came to.

Then the miracle happened. Suddenly it began to turn. Those of you who have witnessed illuminations will recognize this. He suddenly began to raise his head and it was as through it had been dark and suddenly it began to get lighter. I don't mean that it got lighter with him. I mean it began to get lighter in the room. Can you hear me? Did you ever hear the story of Bill Wilson? Bill Wilson, the guy who founded Alcoholics Anonymous, was the worst that had ever been. And the description that the nurse gave at his recovery was that his whole bed was light. It was in 1933. It was witnessed! He was hospitalized for the 28th time, and they said suddenly when he had his experience there was a big light all around his bed. And of course that's what we teach. Anyway, it got brighter and brighter, and his head came up, like that, and it was just like that. The only thing he said was, "I don't have to do this anymore." What he actually said is, "I'm free." And he was. That was it. And in the decade that followed, he became one of the greatest teachers of the fundamental principles of the 12-Step Program without ever divulging that he had been there. He became very famous, calling on people of a particular nature who wanted to hear him.

What did he do the next day? He went to a beginners meeting. He began to make coffee, and he made the beginners meeting his home group. He never progressed past knowing that he had nothing to do with it. Good stuff. We have the kinds of associations that I see here, and I can see you, who know that you didn't have anything to do with this. Can you hear me? You knew that this revelation came for whatever reasons, not depending on you solving your problem, but on your inability to solve it. That's what happened to me.

The rest of my story: I began to have physical manifestations of awakening, as strange as that seems. I began to undergo genuine physical experiences that I had no way of defining, because I had had no experience with what a physical awakening was. Not only was my awakening physical, in one sense it wasn't particularly spiritual. You associate spirituality with Jesus appearing or with reading a scripture. That's really not what happened to me. What happened to me in the beginning was that I got a headache so bad I couldn't stand it. One of those! They took me in an ambulance to the hospital. I had a pressure in my head for no apparent reason, although somewhere I suspected that it might have to do with it, but I wasn't allowed to correlate it. They put me in Hinsdale Hospital. I was living in Naperville, 20 miles west of Chicago, a western suburb of Chicago. I had a couple of acres with horses out there. Boy, my headache got bad. A good friend of mine took one look at me and said, "You're going in the hospital." The pressure was building up, and they ran me through a CAT scan, and it appeared that I had some sort of tumor.

Certainly I had pressure in my head, and my EEG was absolutely wild. It was off the scale. I was having seizures in the middle of my head. They sedated me and they said, "We're going to run some more tests on you tomorrow."

Here I am, under sedation, lying in this hospital in a private room, saying, "How the hell did I get here?" About 2 o'clock in the morning I was awakened by what appeared to be a passage of an energy association across the top of the room. I looked up at it, and it looked down at me and a voice in my mind said, "What's the matter with you?" And I said, "What do you mean what's the matter with me?" (This is in thought.) I said, "I've got this incredible pressure in my head." And he said, "Aw, don't worry about that, that's just a process." That's all he said. "Don't worry about that. That's normal. That's a process." Somebody had forgotten to tell me that. It was like my awakening (transformation) was accidental. And then it dawned on me. I said, "Oh, I'm in a process." And it was gone. All I had to do was make the admission that the occurrence was valid based on something that was happening to me. It began to connect spiritually, perhaps, but at that time it did not. The only problem I had was that I insisted on leaving the hospital at 2 o'clock in the morning. It did not make the doctors and nurses too happy. "Where are you going?" "I'm leaving." "You can't leave here." I found my clothes. It was over and done. And, of course, I was fine.

And I began to have occurrences, and they were physical. My neck got burned, and my fingers all began to burn — all sorts of stuff, which was the sign of the awakening. And I was doing bizarre things because I was beginning to re-image in my mind. I had an image in my mind of a golden walking stick. For whatever reasons, I was shown a beautiful image of a golden walking stick. I didn't know what to do with it. So I decided to form the Peerless Walking Stick Company. The invention of my mind was that I would teach "spiritual walking." I don't know where this came from, but I would sell sticks, and we could communicate with each other by walking and talking, carrying a stick. I made the connection. I designed a beautiful brochure. And I wanted the heads to be beautiful. They were colored, and the 'finial'... I studied all about sticks. There's a great history of walking sticks. I decided I was going to import some special cane, *Ting Ling* cane it's called, which was the best cane you could get. But it came from Communist China. So I got on a plane and I went out to San Francisco. I was nuts. There's no question. For those of you who have had these experiences, it seems so reasonable at the time. And it was reasonable. So I contacted the agency out there for China, and I arranged to import cane. Actually, I did it. I imported it, and I sold a lot of sticks. So I had the Peerless Walking Stick Company.

So I was in downtown San Francisco for some reason or other, I must have been doing pretty well, and I was lying in bed. I had lived in San Francisco for ten years — in suburban San Francisco. I was at KGO in San Francisco in 1950 on television. Then I moved back to the Chicago area. So I'm up in the room, and I'm lying in bed, and all of a sudden I began to have genuine kundalini experiences. Starting at the bottom of my feet, voo-voo-voom, I *really* began to have them. And I knew nothing about it. Nothing. No one had ever told me that somehow there were chakras and about your spinal cord. It felt real good. It felt wonderful. I'm lying there, and it's kind of exciting. Some day I'll tell you about the passion I experienced there. I was not young then. I was a half a century then. You guys don't know how old I am. I'm older than you think. That's a long time ago. I'm talking about 17 or 18 years ago. During the awakening, I would have passionate experiences that were incredible, and they were based on absolutely nothing. You are accustomed to having some sort of passionate interlude that is justified by viewing a picture or seeing somebody. It wasn't true with me. I could be in the middle of a sales meeting and I had people working for me, and all of a sudden the energy would go voo-voo-voom!!

You could feel me — I'll tell you that. I learned very early to be very careful. I was taught to be careful because in the period I went through during my awakening, everybody would give me everything. And I didn't know why. But I could walk into the banker and he would try to loan me money. This is fun. I would sit down, smile, and say, "How are you doing?" and he would say, "How much do you want?" "I don't need any money." "Ah, come on." Something was going on.

And I would have passion. I would actually have total, full ejaculation passion. Oh, yes. They weren't pre-mature at all. In fact, they were very mature. That's kind of funny, isn't it? What am I doing here telling you this? I must be getting ready. My time is very short. Those of you who know me, I've never really told this.

I felt real good, and I was on Market Street in downtown San Francisco. I came out and walked down Powell or Mason. There was a little bookstore, one of the old kind in San Francisco, where there are all sorts of books. I always liked to go in them. They're kind of old-fashioned. And I walked in and I was walking along, not looking for anything, and I glanced up just in time to have a book fall out and hit me on the head. That's a true happening. And I picked it up and it said, *The Kundalini Experience: Psychosis or Transcendence?* It was a book written by some doctor [Lee Sannella]. It actually fell out and hit me on the head. And I said, "Oh, that's what's happening to me! I'm in a kundalini experience. I better tell them it's not psychosis, that it's spiritual." It was probably more psychosis at the time. And that's a strange thing. When I say that happened, everybody goes, "Oh, no it didn't." But it did, although it seemed perfectly natural at the time. My certainty is that you are being guided in this. Like Jesus says, you may hear some very strange things, and you make some very strange requests, but it is impossible that you are not being guided, because you are under the same guide that guided me.

There is no explanation for my illumination, and as it continued, I was illuminate and my death process — what you call death, I don't use the term death — my devastation occurred on the 4th of July, 1979. Those kind of experiences are written about in books but they're not discussed. Obviously I was completely and totally devastated. Everything had been going so well. Everything was going just perfectly for me. I was happy with dogs and horses and my spiritual awakening, and I had begun to read books. I was in my bedroom, and all of a sudden it all caved in. That episode of fear could not be described. I didn't recognize it as death; it was preventing me from dying. There is no way that I could escape it. I tried to get underneath my wall-to-wall carpeting. I had wall-to-wall carpeting and I ripped up the side of the carpet and tried to hide underneath it. It was real interesting. The next morning I was entirely new. I was very certain, but I had no identification with my newness. I can remember about two days later (I was married at the time, and I had a child), we had company over to the house. We were entertaining, and I walked out into the living room (for some reason or another we were talking about the world) and said, "This world isn't real," and everybody turned and looked at me. I said, "Everybody knows this is not a real world." And they said, "What are you talking about?" I said, "The world isn't real. We're all here just doing what we do, and that's perfectly OK, but it's not real." And I began to have difficulties. Obviously.

From that time on, it's pretty intense. Your need to teach it will be pretty intense. So that's what I began to do. As far as the experiences themselves go, presume that they're going to be a part of your awakening. My instructions to you have always been, no matter what happens, no matter how bizarre, no matter how impossible, no matter how joyously happy, no matter how unpredictable they are, accept them as a part of the process, and you will be fine. If you read the preliminary statement in the Endeavor Academy *Out of Time* journal, it will say what I was taught about it. I was taught that it is an evolutionary process. These are direct teachings, and if you've read a lot of my old original writing (*Spiritual Teachers Notebook*), it will say this. The work I did in the first three or four years constitute very lucid descriptions of my mind that I was able to write, and took very much for granted. The idea that I could have done it a year before was absurd. Yet it seemed perfectly natural for me to do that, and I did.

The only explanation I ever got when they operated on my head... Suddenly my head was being operated on, and I could hear. Those of you who have ever had surgery and were conscious knew that the doctors were around you and you were lying in bed and they were operating on you. They were operating on me. Something was happening because I could feel it. And one of them said to the other one, "How's he going?" And the other guy said, "I don't think we can do it." And the other one said, "Why don't you try that?" And he said, "If you do that, he won't be able to see." And amazingly enough he said, "Well, go ahead, that's the best we're going to get." So that was performed on me. The reason I teach 'thought' is that I do not have visible light revelation. That is, I am not suddenly able to see light — or very rarely. If I share with some of my new associations like you would be if you went to light suddenly, you might flash me some light. For me light is thought — dark light. There's really no difference in it, since light is thought anyway. I am able to think blue and give other people blue colors. But I don't see them myself. That, evidently, was the flaw that they said I would have in the procedure that I had. And that's the way it is with me.

But except for that, I learned it all by experience. We used the term "shakti" earlier. I didn't even know what that was. I didn't know that I had it. I didn't know why I went to Unity Church in Chicago. First I went to the Theosophical Society. I discovered Theosophy. The reason I did was that it is connected to Buddhism or kundalini rather than Christianity. My awakening wasn't connected to Christianity. It's kind of fascinating. I went downtown to the Unity Church, I walked in, and the minister said, "Why don't you give the service on Sunday." Those sorts of things have happened to me. In the middle of the service, the transcendental meditators who were sitting in the front row began to have very violent experiences in relationship with me. They began to fly. They had been to Fairfield (Iowa) where they were taught to fly with the Maharishi. They experienced my energy, and suddenly they began to hop way up. And it was a little embarrassing. They were sitting in the lotus position and all of a sudden they began to hop up into the air about 20 feet. And I said, "Oh, what's this? What's the matter with you?" And they were going, "Oh, Master!" They recognized me, even if I didn't.

The reason I couldn't be seduced was I knew damn well I didn't have anything to do with it. How would you seduce me? I got it through the grace of God and surrender and service. All I teach is serve. Give it away and serve. Holy mackerel! So that's what I do. That's pretty much my story. The voices directed me. My original nature was very protective; that is, I didn't even allow tape recorders in my talks. The early tapes that you hear of me were snuck in by a meditator underneath the chair. They're great talks. Some of them are as good as anything — in fact, they're probably better than I do today. For whatever reason, I protected that. For whatever reason, you are now interested in sitting and listening to me tell you this, which is a sign that there has been an integration of the so-called religious idea with the natural function of the emergence of you in a metamorphosis of your physical attainment. Yet it doesn't necessarily have to be connected to a doctrine, but it must be connected personally to a need or dedication to overcome a difficulty that is then overcome and maintained through service, forgiveness and love. That's what I do.

This association could perhaps respond to me in a moment for no reason whatsoever, simply because he would say, "That's what that is. That's the guy." Or they would hear about me and would say, "That's the guy. Where is he?" For no reason whatsoever — not because it had been prophesied. A lot of that happened. Some of you knew instantly that you were going to fulfill your function. It is very interesting that that did not necessarily have to be illuminating. Can you hear this? You could have a perceptual responsibility as a lawyer, or an accountant, or whatever you had to do; you would immediately come in and do that. Those of you who know how this grew will understand that. Some of you knew instantly you had to do that. And you did. And you are recognizable to me, generally by your determination.

What has occurred now for the first time began to happen at what we call time-sufficiency. In any particular association of space-time you reach sufficiency. That means that whatever the correlation of pain and death and chaos with our reality, there is a sufficient number that now justifies the exposure. I'll try that once more for you. My exposure is fundamentally very fearful. The *Course In Miracles* is the most fearful thing that could ever happen to you. It leads you directly into fear. The first chapter says it. That's why nobody does *A Course In Miracles*. The first chapter says this *Course* will lead you directly into fear. How could it not? It's the loss of your own identity. It's an experience of enlightenment. It's walking through the shadow of death. It's going into a Gethsemane. It's being crucified. It's being resurrected. It's all of those things.

Somewhere recently there was a sufficiency of illumination that occurred in the ancillary association that has actually never occurred in the world before. Jesus teaches the idea of multiple saviorship, which is really what I'm expressing to you. That comes about simply because it is impossible to objectify me. I refuse your objectification of me. If I hadn't, I would now be the largest Christian denomination in the Universe. Had I set that up, if I had done that, we would have just been a gigantic establishment. But I didn't do that. I couldn't do that. I didn't want to do that. Why would I want you to do that? Instead I taught that you may do this through this process. And certainly that includes forgiveness and all the things that go with that. I never really taught forgiveness, I taught that this is going to happen to you. Give up and come to God.

Apparently, over a period of all these years, there is what we call a sub-culture listening to these tapes. They don't tell anybody. They just simply listen to them. What they don't really know is that it is accumulative. Each time anyone has an experience, and this includes the *Course In Miracles*, it affects everybody in that relationship. And those who weren't ready yesterday are ready today. I am able to do now, perhaps, with the formulation of the Healing Center, what I would not have done a year ago. To me the idea of healing didn't have a lot of meaning, because I could see everybody healed without all the nonsense of Christian healing. Not that I didn't love it and think it was good, but that was not what I did. I raised the dead. I was a teacher of teachers. I wanted you to come and do your own illumination. When that sufficiency occurred, we took it out into the world. This is directly from Jesus. If you take the *Course In Miracles* out into the world, take it out as healing because healing can be a physical demonstration of the spirituality without the necessity for the complete experience. Did you hear me? That does not mean you don't need the Academy or a place where you can come and complete your own process. But it does mean that you can offer to the world your healing grace through the energy of love that you have gained by your own transformation. That's what we do.

We have a Healing Center, and not very many people come to our Healing Center. But that's suddenly going to change because I'm healing. I am able to do it. So the contact that I make with you now is my allowance for you to accept me in partiality that I formerly never would have done. I'm just giving you the fact of the matter. Do you want to hear this? You can present me now with questions that before I would have said, "You're not listening to me at all, get out of here." That's why they say, "Don't go to him, he'll tell you that you're a dummy." Many of you perhaps are as dumb as you used to be, but perhaps not. That would be because of the sufficiency of the Light energy that has become a part of this. That occurs at what you call this level of association — coming from the medulla oblongata, and it actually occurs in the pineal gland. But instead of teaching simple reflection, I bring it from the pituitary, which actually includes the process from the gonads, directly to the pituitary. So my provision to you contains the Light and also the transformative possibility of your body. Did you hear that? I expressed that in the Eastern association. So when I offer you energy, you may suddenly experience more than you thought you would, simply because I'm an entire activator and am not limiting it to the upper few chakras. I don't know how to express that. That seems to be the case because you may very well begin to have very intense physical experiences.

More than that, this is a contagion of Light. You must understand that this is not all that big a place. There are only five billion of us. There's not that many of us. It's only a little place. When you begin to have the experience, everyone else begins to catch that Light in their association. It's a communicative ease. It can be communicated. In fact, it's easier to communicate than disease itself, because, when the resistance to it is relinquished, it is no longer necessary to set up other protective devices. The resistance of cause and effect is converted to the acceptance of it. In that sense, it's not remedial at all. It is the repair through the RNA to the DNA itself. There was no DNA here originally, it was

RNA. The DNA is a formulation of the feminine association of potential. The message itself is carried by the DNA in the activation of the enzymes that transform your bodily associations contained within...oh, shut up! Who cares? But it *is* glandular. We keep getting calls: "Can I measure your melatonin?" So they've got melatonin and they are producing it artificially and they are using it as a sleep agent. Actually it's a lot more than that. But since the body only accepts it as soothing, it will soothe. There's nothing wrong with it, but the activation could very important to you in your own memory. That's all a part of the healing process.

Does that have to be explained to the people who come to be healed? No. But if I'm explaining it to you, it is probably an indication that you want to know about it. It is probably an indication that you are a teacher or that you have a need to serve, or there is an element in you of service. I say "probably" because I have no way of determining it. Certainly at this level of association we need teachers. We need illuminate associations. But if they disappear from here, if they just leave, what good are they going to do us? Generally speaking, if you have an experience you will begin to carry that message or experience. The manner in which we intend to do this, as I told you earlier, is *A Course In Miracles*.

This is confidential. When I say I am communicating with Jesus, the mind of Jesus, directly, I mean it. I mean that the advice that you are getting is also of that. So let's stop kidding ourselves about the need to say who it is. I couldn't care less who it is. If it is an illuminate voice connected to what you have been looking at in the method of coming to know, which is the direct route — this route — that says, "Don't do anything. Come into this and it is available." Ramana Maharshi. The direct association of samadhi without any of the nonsense. At the very minimum with what you call Aurobindo — Integral Yoga, using your mind and letting yourself come to it. That's what I'm offering you.

Need you know this in order to be healed? No. That lovely mind back there is going to be healed regardless of anything he says. It is impossible that you can be around me and not be healed. But the joy that I'm beginning to experience in it is that there seems to be a very solid indication of a possibility that this association is about to be over. I'm going to say this to you in case you think that there is some way I can explain that. Let me try it this way: Over is over.

I know that you think it ends in some big gigantic catastrophe. It doesn't. It simply doesn't end that way. Because of the nature of your spatial references, if there are too many of you, you will be viewed as an entire failure. Can you hear me? Outcomes are always predicted by what the associations want to see. I'll use the Healing Center. I invite everyone to a final association of the Healing Center and we all come and we say now the portal is going to open up and we're all going to ascend to Heaven at 12 o'clock tonight. Twelve o'clock comes and we ascend to Heaven and are gone. The next morning the people driving by in their cars say, "Oh, there they are, the whole thing failed." Can you hear me? It's the same as though I took twelve of you up to the top of the hill and say we're going to stay up here until God comes. The next day we come down from the hill all disheveled and it didn't work. That's nonsense. They left. You are the one that saw them come down. They're not here. They came down because they are phantom figures of failure in your mind.

It's the same people that saw Jesus crucified on the cross. He wasn't crucified. He's resurrected. Many of you didn't even want to accept Him when He came there and said, "I'm resurrected." Do you hear me? So your scenario is that of washing your hands. Your scenario is that of, "It didn't work." It would have to be, otherwise you wouldn't be here. Sorry about that. That sounds like a cop-out doesn't it? It is a cop-out. The one thing that you can't accept in the healing book, if you're really going to be a healer, is that your healing is perfect all the time. So this is a cop-out. You're going to use it perceptually to say, "Ha, ha, you failed." I didn't fail. When you read our *Miracle Healers Handbook* and it says, "Should Healing Be Repeated?," Jesus says, "What the hell are you talking about? It worked perfectly." It will then say, "Look at yourself." It will then say, "You don't seem to think that attempts to heal again are an attack on God." I don't want to get into it. That can't be understood by the world, and it does not have to be understood by the world. But it *does* have to be understood by you.

It needs to be understood by you because the conversion to phenomena will not solve the problem. It's not going to make any difference at all to the world — not really — if I go to Madison Square Garden and say, "At 12 noon today I am going to energize and disappear." I will do it. I will energize and I will disappear. And it will be good for a story for about three days. Am I right? "Man Disappears." Since it cannot be accepted into the entirety of the association, it becomes an anomaly. All of the definitions for how it occurred need not be true. There will then be people who say: "I saw him pulled out with strings." "It's not true." And all the other reasons why it's impossible that that occurred. If it is totally impossible, it won't be seen at all. Can you hear that? That's quite a step. If it is possible, but cannot be organized into the association, it will simply be rejected. It will not be considered part of the statistical possibility. Since I cannot die and I never get sick, I am not a part of the statistical possibility that organizes whether an 80-year-old man can get sick and die. I'm thrown out of the equation. You can't count me. I'll throw the experiment off. If I'm 460 years old, I don't count. Can you hear that? I can't be considered part of the association. Not that I am; actually I'm about 642 years old.

The persistence of the necessity of the conceptual mind not to acknowledge the miracle is amazing, because it must justify the association in the occupation of its own mind. A good friend of mine who is one of the best surgeons I ever knew, and he still is, and he is beginning to have experiences because I took care of a problem he had, confessed to me, that he was going to do a major stomach tumor (I mean major pancreas/stomach, no hope) surgery on a woman who had what the nurse describes as a spiritual experience the night before in the operating room. He didn't know about it, but they wheeled the woman into the room and the tumor wasn't there. It just wasn't there. Here are the possible reactions. First of all: "I've got the wrong patient." Next: "I've got the wrong X-rays. There must be a mistake in the X-rays." The pursuit of it finally becomes futile. And he looks at his watch, and says, "Well, take her away, I've got another one coming in." That's the way it works. That became an anomaly. Obviously it was not acceptable within the association. I can share this with you. Of the many good doctor friends that I have, most of them know that their patients get better by miracles, not by how they treat them. I don't care whether you want to hear that or not — it's true. What they do is give them medication and pray. I'm talking about real general practitioners. I'm not talking about barbers. I'm not talking about surgeons. To me surgeons are barbers. Medicine is a craft and if a guy needed his leg cut off, he went to a barber because that's mechanical. You give them a remedy and you hope that suits them; and you hope that he recovers rather than killing him. Obviously the remedy you give him is a poison directly connected to the healing — hopefully.

Actually what happens is some doctors heal better than other doctors because they heal with their mind. GPs have a way — are there still any around? Are there General Practitioners? Some of them are quite good. We had a Dr. Layton who was so good all he had to do was show up. Not only was that true, but he knew it. He knew he had to show up, and he would pull up in his car, and get out with his bag and, "Oh, wow, you're finally here, doctor. I'm okay now." What was that? Service! It's nothing but service. It was a dedication. He wanted to make them well. He wished them well. He wanted to help them. His service was not based on monetary concern — at least not too much, not any more than necessary. So it wasn't a form of exchange, it was a form of giving or love. And that's the manner in which real healing occurs, isn't it? Your need to do that.

The intensity with which you are going to begin to express your love through giving is going to surprise you. That may become very passionate for you. This is Jesus. No one was more passionate or determined to teach revelation through the necessity to heal than that mind. So you will be an emulation of that mind. You will be a form of that mind, just as my mind is. I may sit here and begin to just talk to you about that because I want you to have that experience. There is some good pleasure going on concerning the breadth of the awakening that's occurring in this association. It's starting to show up on what we call the "Big Board."

I'm going to try a couple of things with you. This is not a real place. I know that you think somehow that you're spinning around. That's all well and good. But it's not really true. At any moment you may simply decide that the dream is over, and the dream is going to be over for you. I'm telling you that, as a fact of your own association. You should start to hear it. I know it is outrageous. I know it's impossible. I know it's mystical. I know all the reasons you can give me objectively for it. They have absolutely no meaning to me at all. I am speaking to you from a certainty that there is no such place as this. I almost immediately apologize for you being here, which is what I'm doing now. I'm sorry. I am sorry for this. I am talking directly to you.

I better tell you this: When I ask for an explanation of why I am able to do this without any apparent historic reference, I am told that I am a substitute. I am told that I am an insertion. I know this is true, if you would like to hear it. I am an insertion of a pattern of converting energy because your other savior didn't make it. I don't know how to explain this to you. But the assignment that was supposed to be performed failed. Krishnamurti appears to be who it was. At the time of the illumination of Krishnamurti, he was picked to be the connection between the East and the West, as I understand it. I'm just picking this up. He was spotted by Annie Besant. They saw him as a six-year-old and they saw his illuminate possibilities and he was taught to be the Christ. The problem that he had was that he was so fraudulently presented as the Christ. To be presented as the Christ when there is no verification for it in your own mind is not acceptable. And it just missed. Are you familiar with him? He's a beautiful, loving consciousness who, as I am doing now, would sit on the stage and say, "Look at it, look at it." But he could never offer his entirety. The rejection of that occurred at a carnival in 1936 when he got sick and tired of being presented as the Christ, particularly when he was being presented in a fraudulent manner, although that's the nature of it. I think that was Leadbeater and a couple of other guys. He absolutely rejected it. From that moment on he became a great spiritual teacher.

The energy of Krishnamurti probably would have lasted about 246 years because it was a step using physical transformation to include Christianity. To take the jump that you are taking with me to the actual physical resurrection of the body, and use the term "you must be born again" of 2000 years ago, is very difficult. But that's what I'm telling you. So the *Course In Miracles* is the outcome of that, and the *Course* said we're going to put this in now even though you're not ready for it. The *Course* actually says that. The situation is that you are missing a symbol that you can use to represent you, compared to Jesus, to model yourself off of. That's not there. So the *Course* was put in with the out-of-body experience of Jesus which is 2000 years old.

To try to make that connection is virtually impossible for you because you have no bridge for it. You couldn't use the connection of kundalini and awakening. That's what I am. I promise and guarantee you that although I'm using the faculties of a guy who was born and raised here, I am not from here. I am not from here. I can remember what this consciousness went through that justified or qualified me. And I can tell you stories about devastation — I was at the atomic bomb area after the bomb. I have all of that as part of my nature. But that's not the reason for my illumination. It is the reason why I was chosen to be illuminated. I was simply the most likely prospect. If you run everything through the computer (this is the way it works), you can turn up associations that for whatever reasons are justified in doing what they do. The stories that I have told you obviously qualify me. I saw my best friends killed. I killed other associations. I had battles, I had rage, I had passion, I was very young — on and on. And I'm old. I can remember these associations very well. That's why I have that.

So the memories that I present you with are human memories, but if you listen to me I positively am a ringer. The importance of that is this: Multiple saviorship will progress much more rapidly if you will accept a ringer, because there is no way that you can justify me in your historic reference. I'm not in it. So I can jump immediately to the necessity for your Christhood, which is exactly what I'm doing. I am not denying you the process by which I came to know it, but I am denying my Christhood in relationship with the provincialism of what you are in becoming Christ. I look at you as provincial. I look at you as historic references of localities that are undergoing the experience. What are we going to have? Multiple saviors. That's at least 500 years off. And you are going to emerge very rapidly, that is, the idea in the *Course* where you would stand up and say, "I am the savior of the world," without using a model. You used me, but I didn't let you. You used me and all I expressed was my own certainty of your perfection. When I explained to you how I came about, I laid no claims to it being doctrinal at all because it wasn't. Isn't that amazing?

So in those first few years I went back and saw all of these things happen. What surprised me the most is nobody would accept what they were teaching. So I had to take what you had taught and rejected and offer it to you anew simply because it was true. For me it is astonishing that you can now pick up the teachings of Jesus, which are so obvious if you would look at them, that everyone has denied for two thousand years, and now you can see it. The reason you can is that you are undergoing your own illumination.

I understand that you may well idolize me and that's perfectly OK. I'm going home anyway. You can now reject me and say, "Well, you didn't get it by any means; therefore I don't want anything to do with you, because I believe that it's necessary for me to have means to do it." If you ask me how to do it, I'll say things like serve, give everything away and let's get the hell out of here. This is Ramana Maharshi. I have absolutely no concern about the method that you come to do it. I will, if you will allow me to, provide you with all the necessary accoutrement of Light that will justify your leaving here with no necessity for any residual at all. You will not have to repeat it. Thank you!

Those of you who can hear this, here's what happens: Most of you are actually leaving and coming back. They don't know it; they may know it. When they come back they're just immediately in the association. I could leave here (and did just then), and come back any time I wanted, and it will be exactly the same time it was when I left. Can you hear that? It's like scribing the *Course*. When you turn it on, it's just going to keep right on saying what it's been saying for the last thousand years. It doesn't matter where it is; it will just pick up right at that moment.

If I pick up a lesson — these are the lessons of the Workbook — and I wanted to have a *Jesus Is Praying* book, this *Jesus Is Praying* book is invaluable. The *Miracle Healers Handbook* and all of them are wonderful things to have. I did the central thought for you. The central thoughts are: there is no world; there are no degrees of miracles; all power is given unto you; and the decision is yours. Isn't that fun? Here's Lesson 163: It says, "There is no death. The Son of God is free." Does that mean there is no death? It means there is no death and the Son of God is free!

> *Death is a thought that takes on many forms, often unrecognized.* Is that so? Death takes on forms. *It may appear as sadness...* Is that death? *...fear, anxiety or doubt; as anger...* Is anger death? Yes! Any formulation of anything in your association is literally a denial of the perfection of your own mind, if you'd like to hear it. *...faithlessness and lack of trust; concern for bodies, envy...* Death is concern for bodies? He doesn't leave anything out in there. The only thing we want to impress on you with this is that you are dead. Every act that you perform, including what you think you love, is only love of death. Okay, we've got that. I'll finish it. *...and all forms in which the wish to be as you are not may come to tempt you. All such thoughts are but reflections of the worshipping of death as savior and as giver of release.*

There is almost no one in this room that somewhere along the line has not said, "I'll be glad when this is over. I've just had enough of this. I wish I was dead." So you go off somewhere and die a little bit and then come back and face the problem some more.

> *Embodiment of fear, the host of sin, god of the guilty and the lord of all illusions and deceptions, does the thought of death seem mighty.*

Are you ready? Death is the lord of all illusions and deceptions.

Death is the devil of your mind. Death is what you bow down to and worship as a real incredible power which can influence you. Do you see that? You are what? An advocate and an adherent of death. Obviously death as God can have no power unless you empower it. Your advocacy of the devil or death is what death is. Death alone would be totally meaningless. Notice the difference between death and God. God is an eternal association Who is real despite your advocacy. I'm just telling you the fact of the matter. God is going to be God. He does not require a definition of Himself in correspondence. Death does. I'm giving you the fact of the matter. All you have to do at any moment in your mind is to say, "Death, I'm not going to pay any attention to you anymore." All of the forms that are apparently represented here are a part of the nature of death worship. We don't do human sacrifice much any more, do we? Do you still do human sacrifice? Sometimes you do. You don't eat each other any more, do you? You do sacrifice each other for love. At some high level, you sacrifice yourself to death, and "greater love hath no man than to die for his brother." And that's very valuable and it's very honorable because everything you do is honorable. But the fact of the matter is that it is to death. Finally you're not going to do it any more. It doesn't make any sense.

The thought of death seems mighty. This is what got me into that little discussion with Gangaji. I really love her. I've got to clear that out for you. I don't want anyone to think I don't love Gangaji and Papaji. What I am teaching is obviously Ramana Maharshi. I do not want the advocacy — this would be true of Jesus Christ — of the association of any teacher of God to be reduced to a justification for death. Is that okay with you? I have to tell you this because I am told to do it. I don't know whether that bothers you or not. The same problem exists in Christianity. I don't want the Christian to tell me that somehow I have to die in order to find enlightenment; that somehow I have to model myself physically in a physical death association. Usually where the problem will occur, and certainly it occurs with this association, is she will connect the need for ego death to the need for physical death. Obviously Ramana teaches, "I died." It had nothing to do with his body at all because from that moment on he said, "There is no world." If there is no world, the idea of body death is totally meaningless. This is *A Course*

In Miracles. The idea that you would actually rot and get old and die is not contained anywhere in his teaching or in Jesus' teaching.

Here's what happened here. The association sees pain and death, which is the human condition. It also is teaching the teachings of Ramana, who says you must have a death experience, so she teaches that he had a death experience instead of a life experience. He may describe it as death, as Paul says, "I die daily." I die all the time. But that's not the expression of death; that's an expression of life. If it is an expression of death, it would indicate that death somehow has a power that can be asserted over you that is necessary for you to experience life — as though there is some sort of combat going on in you. It is not true!

What it results in is the necessity for you to accept in your mind that the loved ones that you are experiencing that are dying of cancer are necessary as a part of your own illumination. I can't accept it. That is not acceptable to me. It is just not fair. I understand that you're going to love them, but I cannot understand the necessity to get old and suffer and die in order that I may use it for the progress of my own awakening. The reason I had to do that is that I don't want anyone to be misled — and certainly Papaji is not. Any problem these associations have will always be physical resurrection. And that doesn't concern me at all. This is a lovely little book. I had never seen it. She's beautiful. There's her picture, and she has a lot of lovely energy. But she says here, "I went to the funeral." She's talking about going to a funeral and having an experience of death. She says, "What you are speaking of now is sensing the power of death coming toward you." That is not acceptable to me. There is no way I'm going to empower death at all. "...the power of death coming toward you. Death is all around. Whenever there is birth there is death." I don't know what that means, but for me whenever there is birth there is eternal life. Sorry!

Here's the real problem: "A meeting with death is your opportunity." Her mother suffered a lot of pain and was dying. "This time with your mother can be a time of rejoicing." I couldn't. I can't. You can't sell me on that. I am allowed to have the pain that I'm feeling. I'm going to connect that pain to the reality of my transformation, but it's not going to justify it. "This time with your mother can be a time of rejoicing. Why else do you think death exists?" I don't know what that has to do with Ramana Maharshi. I'm going to tell you what it has to do with it: Nothing! "Why else do you think death exists?" So that we can witness it and justify the pain and the necessity to overcome it? I have no objection. There is no objection to teaching this. There is an objection coming from that entire cycle that says, "Don't teach that's what I say." Incidentally that came directly from Ramana who is my beautiful, dearly-beloved whole mind who teaches exactly what I'm teaching — and did, and does. "Why else do you think death exists? If there were no death, what a missed opportunity this would be to experience what does not die." I don't understand. "What is untouched by ill-health, birth, death, coming and going appearance. Death is a powerful utility for realization." Nonsense! Nonsense! Don't you believe that for one second. Don't you dare do that with me! Don't you dare justify death by telling me that somehow once you do that you're going to be able to experience. Don't you do it. Ramana says absolutely that death is impossible because this entire association is not what Life is at all. I was supposed to do that. That's the end of that. Bless her heart.

Question: You yourself said that your utter devastation got you to the point where you experienced the illumination.

That's what I am speaking of when I'm speaking of the death of the ego. But it has absolutely nothing to do with physical death. Her whole problem is that she has connected it with the physical death of the body. It is not connected to the body at all. It is the transformation of the body through the realization, not the death of the body. Is this what happened in Christianity? Sure. It's exactly the same thing that they're doing with Jesus in Christianity — which is fine. That objection came from a very high source. I'm not too familiar with those associations except as I meet the Eastern meditators' minds who are willing to look at me. Many of them are very joyous and they have lovely contacts of forgiveness and love. I would not want that to be the doctrine of their teaching, because it is not true. This is particularly important now, and then we'll end this. Don't empower death! If you let death have power over you, it will exercise it because you have given it the power to do so. Do you hear me? Death is an idea. You bet your boots it is. Swear not to die, you holy son of God, you made an agreement that you can't keep.

> *The frail, the helpless and the sick bow down before death's image, thinking it alone is real, inevitable, worthy of their trust. For it alone will surely come.*

Would you bow down to idols such as this? Here is the strength and might of God Himself perceived within an idol made of dust. Here is the opposite of God proclaimed as lord of all creation, stronger than God's Will for life, the endlessness of love and Heaven's perfect, changeless constancy. Here is the Will of Father and of Son defeated finally, and laid to rest beneath the headstone death has placed upon the body of the holy Son of God.

Unholy in defeat, he has become what death would have him be. His epitaph, which death itself has written, gives no name to him, for he has passed to dust. It says but this: 'Here lies a witness that God is dead. Because you are God's son dead.

If you are the perfect living Son of God; if you have allowed your brother to die, you are saying that God is dead. That is an amazing idea. *And this it writes again and still again, while all the while its worshippers agree, and kneeling down with foreheads to the ground, they whisper fearfully that it is so.* Yet the worshippers are never successful in dying. We can go to funerals. You and I can go and love each other and watch them lay our dear friend down in the grave. And we can say together what a wonderful association we had together. And that's all true. And now he is lost to us. And finally we are going to be lost in the same amnesia and death that's going to swallow us up. Dust to dust. Ashes to ashes. Till death do us part. Don't do that!

That doesn't mean that you don't go to the funeral. Go to the funeral and discover that he's standing right next to you. That's one of my great experiences. John O'Malley. How I loved him. He was a guy that didn't make it. He was an Irishman. He suffers from the Irish disease. No matter how many times he got it, he never got it. He just couldn't get it, and he finally just died of alcoholism. One of the sweetest, most wonderful blarney Irish guys — great joke teller. Of course all of the Program people went to his funeral. His mother was there. One of the alkies went up to her and said, "We're so sorry about John. Too bad he never got the Alcoholics Anonymous Program." And his mother said, "Oh, he wasn't that bad." Somehow he didn't really need the Program. And the guy was gone! It's typical of your defense against death. So I'm standing there and all of a sudden he's standing right next to me. It was a real funny experience, because I must have called on that guy a million times.

I bailed him out of jail. He had six kids. And he was a hard worker, but when he went, he would go entirely. Did you ever hear of being struck drunk? He could be entirely sober and everything was going along beautifully — the better it got, the more likely he was to have a slip — finally things would be going so good that he wouldn't turn into the bar, his truck would. He would swear to me that he went on by, but his truck turned in, and some other guy got out and went in and had a drink — but it wasn't him. In one particular sense, it wasn't him. Anyway, John was standing next to me, and he looked, and he said, "How do I look?" I said, "Just fine." What a lovely guy. He was never mean. When he was drunk he was the nicest guy you'd ever know. Wow! To be powerless and not be able to do anything about it is incredible. We've got you, guys, don't you worry.

It is impossible to worship death in any form, and still select a few you would not cherish and would yet avoid, while still believing in the rest. For death is total. Either all things die, or else they live and cannot die. No compromise is possible. Life is eternal. What appears to be death is only a change to another form of life. Do you hear me? The change to another form of life that is occurring in you now is not death; it is Life. If it manifests itself as the destruction of the body within the form, be not concerned about that in your own relationship with yourself. It is indeed the resurrection. And that's the experience that you are having here with me now.

For here again we see an obvious position, which we must accept if we be sane; what contradicts one thought entirely can not be true, unless its opposite is proven false. Once more, I don't want to make this hard for you since you are hearing me. There is an eternal loving Eternal Life. This is a place where there is pain and death. This is not real. That's why I want you to deny death. Why? It is not real. Any manifestation of space-time will be a form of a beginning and an end. Any manifestation. "In the beginning, God created Heaven and earth." Is that so? When is it going to end? Never. Then why did it begin? I don't know. But anything that has a beginning will have an end. That's not what Life is, because Life is eternal. All of the other questions are valid: "How did I get here? Where am I going? What's going to happen?" I don't know. But if I can show you the simplicity of the eternity of Life compared to the split condition of your own mind, you can choose to be eternal, very simply because that's what you are. And that's the solution that I am offering you now in your own mind. Does it seem not to have any correspondence with time? It doesn't!

But what I'm curious about, if this is true, what possible connection would time have with eternity? Does eternity wait to be eternal until time decides it is? Jesus says that eternity is going on exactly the way it is when you made the sojourn into death. Nothing has changed at all. You came in, and you're going to leave, and you are going to be home. Won't that be nice?

Death's worshippers may be afraid. And yet, can thoughts like these be fearful? If they saw that it is only this which they believe, they would be instantly released. And you will show them this today. And that's what I intend to show you. *There is no death, and we renounce it now in every form, for their salvation and our own as well. God made not death. Whatever form it takes must therefore be illusion. This the stand we take today. And it is given us to look past death, and see the life beyond.*

Is this what I said to read at all funerals? Yes! I got this to be read at funerals because it acknowledges eternal life at the grave site:

> *Our Father, bless our eyes today. We are Your messengers, and we would look upon the glorious reflection of Your Love which shines in everything. We live and move in You alone. We are not separate from Your eternal life. There is no death, for death is not Your Will. And we abide where You have placed us, in the life we share with You and with all living things, to be like You and part of You forever. We accept Your Thoughts as ours, and our will is one with Yours eternally. Amen.*

Where did that come from? Do you know the guy that wrote that prayer? He's your best friend. He's standing right next to you now.

This story is about over. This is the story that will be told in space-time for the next thousand years. The story I told you today, I'm sure somebody is going to figure it out and tell the story. I don't care. They're going to discover this insertion, and they're going to discover the formulation of healing centers, and they're going to discover my lucid teaching of quantum in association with time, and all of the stuff that we have done together in our dedication to escape it, and it's going to become more and more commonplace in the nature of you coming from death to Life.

Sometimes at the end of these sojourns we experience a sort of nostalgia. It's like: Now that it's over, it was OK. All of the screw-ups and the stuff that we went through, forget it. All of the mis-adventures and all of the mis-communications. Jesus says in the *Course* that it's an incredible happening. It couldn't have happened, but it apparently did. I am happy to be able to report that the connection is intact. The reason that you can leave is because the function of the completion of the association of resurrection, or a path from time to eternity, is becoming available.

First of all, what we did was establish a fast lane because of the clog — the slowness of the super-highway, what you call the "King's Highway." It just clogged up because no one was entirely sure that they wanted to go to it. If you don't have clear vision up ahead, you have a tendency to take one step up and two steps back. So the highway has been clogged up. Generally speaking, the first thing we did was give you a fast lane where you could drive along the outside of it. That did not complete the process, but it enabled you to go up the side, at least get ahead of 500 years, get out and begin to direct traffic to get out of the way for those who were being clogged up by the associations that didn't want to hear this. Or, perhaps, to invite some fellow travelers, who wondered what the hell was going on, to ride up with you and come out and take a look at the result, because they could see immediately that getting in that mess wasn't what they wanted to do. That's a fact. I don't know how else to explain this. I'm just talking energy here.

The other answer was to evolve, as some of us have, simply another way out. You may believe that the only way out of this is the King's Highway. That is not true. There has always been available in space-time continuum what we call worm holes, or methods by which you can move directly through time to another association. We used to think of them as back doors that we would climb, or places behind other associations that we could go to. So some of you have learned methods of literally disappearing from the earth for as long a period as you want to, and then returning to fulfill a particular function. This is going to happen more and more in this world as more and more of you become necessary in specific reassociations for specific jobs. You may call them angels if you wish. They are a step above an angel because they are fully facilitated to perform any act necessary, where an angel is a thought of a particular necessity that is expressed by your desire in limitation. What it says is this: If you are at any moment ready to meet the Christ, He can appear for you around the corner as a peanut vendor, and rather than having to offer you a bag of peanuts on the house and communicate with you something that you are ready to hear, which is what an angel would do... If you came around the corner and needed to know something, somebody might suddenly hand you a slip of paper. Obviously it would be an angel that's offering you a solution. It's very possible for you to meet your own association that's telling you directly that it is time for you to do this. It is time for you to take your place as the savior.

Obviously what I'm trying to do is express what is not expressible. But it is 'experienceable,' and certainly any story that you want to tell about it is fine with me. It will be a drama of you coming here, being here and coming home. And it will include the method by which you came home, even though the method is not real and requires a recognition of you individually. How else would it be if God is in everything you do and always present? You must be shown that in a method that is acceptable to you. And that's what we are doing now.

Discourse with Master Teacher

Ever Present

However far I wander
He's always there
Waiting for me.

Infinitely patient
Judging me not…
Loving me.

Like a patient Father
Watching, always watching
Me play with my toys
and joys and sorrows.

He calls to me
I tell Him, later…
I'm busy now
With my nothingness.

Until I tire of it all
And seek Him in the dark
Place when all is quiet.

He just shines on me
Exposing my fraudulence
Ignoring my ambivalence.

He speaks to me softly
And calls to me inviting me
To come to the oasis where he lives
I don't always answer
I have things to do
Places to go.

I take Him for granted
I know He's always there.
He doesn't care
What I do
What I think
He lets me be anything I want
And takes joy in my joy.

He inspires and lifts me high
Like a kite in the summer wind
And plays with me and
Delights with me
And when I crash and burn
He gives me balm
And comforts me.

When I get lazy and defiant
He nudges me
And whispers there's more
There is so much more.
Come to the keep.
I close my eyes and
Go back to sleep.

Like a wide open screen
Clean, pristine, loving
He opens to me and
I throw images like mud
Obscuring the beauty
The limitless beauty.

He doesn't care
He lets me project everything
Pretty scenes, ugly scenes, violence,
blood and death.

He is the light
Shining through my
Butterfly wings
As I emerge from my cocoon
I cannot grasp
The awesome wonder of it.

Gardens and oceans and happy children
The starving and the war weary
Suffering and pain and
Horrid little things scampering
Around in the dark avoiding
The light, allowing me to play it out.
To suffer and complain.

And when I get tired and hurt
From all the tiresome projections
He's there, still smiling
Pleased because I am
Myself. He helps me always
When I think to ask
In unfathomable ways
That I cannot mistake the Majesty.

And sometimes, sometimes he catches me
Unawares and plunges me
Into the boundless expanse
And gives me a taste of the eternal Now
Beyond my senses
Beyond my mind
Beyond my comprehension
Leaving me a beggar at heaven's gate.

And I, the Progenitor of all that is and ever was
Marvel at the power and the glory
Humbled in the awareness
That the ever changing is
As well the Ever Present
And to my incredulous surprise
None other than my Self.

Pat Connor

Orchid Fantasy Leda Robertson

Dear Reader...

I went for a walk the other evening, apparently alone on an empty country road. Soft flakes of snow were falling and the trees enveloping the road were caressing each flake as they floated by. All sound was dampened by the new blanket of snow. And, in my mind, I invited you along. Very soon, I was flooded by an intense phenomenon, now very familiar and welcome to me, but once very terrifying. In the beginning, I associated it with you: both in the suppressed rage I held against you for abandoning me to that bottomless pit of emptiness and loss I was experiencing; and in the yearning evoked by the memory of those quiet, passionate moments we had known that embraced the entire universe, that transcended our body limitations, and which contained a familiar intimacy of communication that reached into our inner soul and turned us inside out.

But this snowy night the passion was Total. Gone were the associations of injury and grievances done to me. Gone was the sorrow of human love known and lost. Gone even was the story of you and me. There was only a vibrancy of sensation that intensified to a thrilling, electric, dissolving of the distinction between body, mind, and heart. Gone were the trees, the road I was walking on, even the body I had located myself in. I knew only the ecstatic merging with the Christ that you walking with me had now become. And that. . . words cannot express.

Knowing You as who You are in Reality also has shown me what Everything is, including Myself, because I could not know You as the Christ without first recognizing it in myself. For that, Dear Reader, I am eternally grateful.

While you may object to my making this story personal to you, I must tell you gently, you are wrong. Whomever I was thinking about that evening had to be you, since my revelation if true would have had to include you. The very essence of Singular Reality is its All-Encompassing Nature. Conversely, the character of the mind in separation is its exclusion. Transformation then, would begin with your willingness to be included in or the recognition by you of the need for your own transformation.

This epistle is an invitation to activate the transformative process in you. It is not by any means a treatise promoting religious doctrine. Yet, the experience I invoke is a profoundly spiritual one in that it is the ecstatic merging of You with the Energy and Love of the Universe of Thought creating. Universal Mind, or God, is what you are. What a Joyful, Exciting discovery to remember that you are not bound by the conflict you perceive constituting the world you see.

Yes, dear Reader, there is actually possible an experience of evolution of the mind that leads to Enlightenment or the remembrance of the Truth of Your Own Singular Reality. Yes, dear Reader, there is a training of mind that works to shift your perception from a presumption of suffering, pain, or loss to a Wholeness of Being that transcends the limitation of vision I have constructed as my self-identity.

Nearly 2000 years ago an enlightened teacher wandered the roads around Galilee and taught that this world was an illusion and that direct contact with God and the remembrance of Reality could be gained through the action of forgiveness in the mind and through the relinquishment of the self-identity. He has returned as he promised he would to teach again the mechanism of Enlightenment through an incomparable *Course In Miracles*.

The impact of *A Course In Miracles* on the evolutionary consciousness of man has been limited by only one factor: the failure of the human consciousness to attribute to the *Course* the possibility of Total transformation to Enlightenment.

The purpose of this paper is to witness in my own Enlightenment that possibility and to demonstrate how the application of the workbook lessons of the *Course* in an uncompromising manner actually corrects perception from multiplicity to a Oneness or At-Onement with the Universe.

"Transformation" is the current buzzword employed by anyone selling anything. It can refer to change in anything from transvestites to corporate structure. And, you can be certain there will be someone selling the means to whatever the end. The word, "transformation", like any idea representing an experience of Totality, has been minimized in meaning in this world until it has, for all intents and purposes, become meaning less.

So, how, in this infinite maze of advertisement for change, can a vehicle for TRUE TRANSFORMATION be recognized for what it is? An expression of Truth would have to express the dilemma exquisitely and so it does: A universal theology is impossible, but a universal experience is not only possible but necessary. It is this experience toward which the *Course* is directed. Here alone consistency becomes possible because here alone uncertainty ends.

Glad Hancock

Journey Without Distance

Needin' things to change
My life to rearrange
Nothin' seemin' lyrical
I'm lookin' for a miracle
Lookin' here and there
Searchin' everywhere
Then came a big surprise
Jesus opened up my eyes

Gettin' down with Jesus
Now I have one purpose
Doesn't cost a single cent
Dancin' in the present
No longer malcontent
Never have to dissent
It's a whole new segment
In this great experiment

In this journey without distance
Gave up all of my resistance
Acceptance is the way to live
That and learning how to give
Now my mind has been released
And I feel eternal peace
Praising Jesus in the light
Everyday and every night

Doesn't matter who you were
Now the past is all a blur
Include yourself in this great story
Feel His Power and His Glory
As you take your brother's hand
Right here in the borderland
Forgiveness ending this illusion
Sets us free of all confusion

The real world comes to
meet our sight
We join together in the light
Perception takes a final bow
Truth experienced here and now
This bright and real association
Brought about our resurrection
Now the fun has just begun
God bless us each and everyone

Nancy Reid

God Is In Everything I See

Oh my God, I thought, "I can just sit on a chair, eat an apple, wear a shirt, drive a car and pass by another human being on the street." I assumed that is what they were for. I was so wrong! I was simply afraid.

And now I can hear the Voice saying: "There is nothing to fear. God is in everything you see." I respond with disbelief: "What do you mean? I know that this chair is a chair. It is hard, angular and motionless. Look, I can sit on it." And there I sit. "Phew… What a relief! Once again I proved to myself that I was a body. It doesn't matter that I am afraid. At least I can hang on to something that is known to me so well." And therefore I get used to my chair. I get used to my fear.

The Voice patiently repeats: "God is in everything you see." I have my ears plugged. And I sit in fear that I will have to eventually get up. And I eat an apple, because if I don't, I will get hungry. And I put on my shirt to cover up my fear with its color and cut. And I enter my car and drive, hoping that the truck from the opposite lane will stay on its side of the road. And I spend the rest of my day bypassing everyone and everything in order to keep my own self-identity.

What is my self-identity? — The defense against everything. I have to defend myself, for if I didn't, I would no longer be myself. I would be everything. I would be God. Brr… It's horrible.

Consequently, I think I am myself because I am not something else. I am not a chair, I am not an apple, I am not a shirt, I am not a car, I am not another guy. I do not see the whole but only bits and pieces. I am but a piece among pieces. No wonder I became a subject for jokes in the universe: "There was a man, he did not know who he was, because he thought he was something else than everything." Ha, ha, ha! What a strange and stubborn creature!

Well, it is not so funny to me. The defense against everything and everyone is a very serious occupation, requiring all of my time and energy.

I hear the Voice again: "You defend nothing against nothing." Now I am getting irritated. "What do you mean I defend nothing? Look at all my achievements. I defend the whole heritage of civilization. If it were not for me, if it were not for a civilization, there would not be any chair, apple, shirt, car, or even another guy. See?! What will you say to that, Voice?"

Silence.

"Ha! See, I won! You will not take away from me what is mine. Now I can sit on my chair until my death. Now I can eat my apples until I am full, and you won't take away from me my intestine cancer. I can even iron my shirt for my own funeral. I can even fly into the universe, only to burn or freeze before I reach the nearest star. See, I can continue to discover new methods of dying with my fellow human beings. Isn't that fascinating?"

Silence…

"Wait a minute. What am I defending? Is it possible that I am defending death?" For everything that I see, even the most beautiful, is doomed to decay and to be annihilated. If I hold on to my perception of the chair as a separate thing, I am willingly condemning myself to death. For if it is separate, I must be separate, too. And if I am separate and apart from the entirety of everything, then I must die. What is the sense in life based on dying? Hmm… I think I don't like this scenario anymore. Maybe life really doesn't have anything to do with what the body's eyes see… Maybe there is indeed another way of seeing and experiencing everything…

Maybe God is in fact in everything that I see…

Oh God, thank you!

Wow! How beautiful! What a joy! What a surprise… Greater joining… There is nothing to defend myself from. There is nothing out there. Everything is here. Everything is in my mind. Everything is everywhere. I am beginning to lose my fear. I am beginning to see the Universe…

Rafał Wereżyński

Searching for a Teacher of Truth

At first I didn't believe you, Teacher,
But we have met before.
"Where?"
Everywhere.
"What time?"
All time. Every time. This time.
Now.
"Who else was there?"
You tell me everyone has been
marked "present."
Everyone holds a ticket stub
Exactly the same as mine.
"How many in line for the Answer?"
Only one?
"Sure?"
I remember the time when I met you,
Teacher.
Viking Theatre. 1954.
You, in no seat, beside me.
"Anything more?"
On the screen old news clips
between Walt Disney and twenty
cartoons.
This day they were showing
Auschwitz
(I was twelve years old).
Thousands of torn bodies, naked
On earth-turned shores,
The bulldozers bruising them swiftly
Into a common grave.

Every dead body was mine
And every dead body was yours
And the world was insane.
"No one comes searching for no
reason.
Why are you here?"
All of us must have experienced
That moment. Together. Alone.
Insanity recognized once and for all.
But there, in the dark, the next reel
Was misplaced in the movie-house
shuffle,
the cry of a prince—abandoned.
Midnight, after all.
"Whose insanity is it?"
Dear Teacher, remember the dark?
Walt Disney couldn't reason,
Or twenty cartoons provide
A child's heart with answers.
So the theatre gave us more—
A free, invisible pass to the pain of
not knowing,
As we exited a thousand theatre doors
Yearning for deliverance and truth.

I wonder, can you guide us, Teacher?
You say you have met us all before.
We, still clutching one glass slipper.
This place. No time. Now.

Pamela Schueller

Flying Machine Lily Bonnes

Creation's Knowledge of Love and Its One Meaning

We are here at the No-Regrets Café and are enjoying coffee and cake, presentations of arts and simple conversations. I want to share with you the art of preparing a cup of divine Cappuccino or Latte and our revelatory mind.

I will try to have a fresh grind of select roasted coffee beans, enticingly aromatic, and dispense the right amount for a single or double shot into the espresso machine's portafilter. The right tamping of the coffee in the portafilter will be reflected in a twenty to thirty second brewing cycle, essential for receiving a perfect espresso shot. This espresso shot is the quintessence of our divine coffee tasting experience.

But before I start the brewing cycle I will already prepare micro-foamed milk or soymilk that becomes the satisfaction for a pleasurable coffee experience. It's funny what foamy steamed liquid can do! This is accomplished through lowering the pitcher until the steam wand rests just below the surface of the milk, and listening to the sound as the steam pours into the milk. It's all in the sound. Amazing! I only have to listen!

Having reached the desired temperature, the steaming process is done. Before setting down the pitcher, I swirl it and gently tap it on the towel-lined countertop, to get a drier foam. I pour the wet micro-foamed milk with just a cap of foam over the espresso shot and offer you a Latte. Or instead, to make a Cappuccino, I can divide the cup into three thirds: one is the shot of espresso, the next is steamed milk, and the last third is the foam. We can finish it with a sprinkle of some cocoa or cinnamon powder on top. With increasing experience we can add some latte or cappuccino art, using the fine tip of cocktail stick or similar tool to draw hearts, flowers, trees or abstract art on top of the foam.

The real Art and creative Action is an expression of our mind thinking with the Mind of God, not just a well-made cup of coffee. Søren Kierkegaard said once: "I see it all perfectly; there are two possible situations – one can either do this or that. My honest opinion and my friendly advice is this: do it or do not do it – you will regret both." But this is the "No Regrets" Café!

We have formed here a circle to come together and give thanks to God and HIS hallowed Creation, to the Son of God, to my Self, to you and to everyone joining this circle which expands without end. We offer gifts to HIM and to each other so that, individually recognized, we can leave the world of our own making, and have perception that is based on fear and separation transformed into Christ's Vision. We are offering gifts from Out-of-time because we have received them by HIM Who knows us perfectly. Each and everyone has a need to cross the borderline of all human ego-based perceptions with all its regrets to the realization of a new, real world.

In Chapter 18 of A Course in Miracles, Jesus calls these the "circle of fear" and the "world of Light."

> *The circle of fear lies just below the level the body sees, and seems to be the whole foundation on which the world is based. Here are all the illusions, all the twisted thoughts, all the insane attacks, the fury, the vengeance and betrayal that were made to keep the guilt in place, so that the world could rise from it and keep it hidden.*

Fear is an illusion. Ralph Waldo Emerson said: "With the past, I have nothing to do; nor with the future. I live now. All life is an experiment. The more experiments you make the better."

What do you use time for? Time is your memory of the past. You are using the past to make yourself happy or unhappy and to feel bound by illusions. Time is of your own making, your toy with which you play the game of a human existence in a dream world that you have dreamed a long time ago. The truth is: You are timeless, eternal – time does not exist. You are the one eternal Being, and eternity is the realization that there is no time, neither passes sequentially. Let us remember together and share the truth as expressed in this incredible Course:

> *This world of Light, this circle of brightness is the real world, where guilt meets with forgiveness. Here the world outside is seen anew, without the shadow of guilt upon it. Here are you forgiven, for here you have forgiven everyone. Here is the new perception, where everything is bright and shining with innocence, washed in the waters of forgiveness, and cleansed of every evil thought you laid upon it. Here there is no attack upon the Son of God, and you are welcome. Here is your innocence, waiting to clothe you and protect you, and make you ready for the final step in the journey inward. Here are the dark and heavy garments of guilt laid by, and gently replaced by purity and love.*

Be happy now. Let's live in the fullness of Creation, the Self we share with God.

Devavan

Thought Collage

Snippets of memory,
wisps of thought
is all that is left
of what time wrought

A sequence is closing
a new scene appears
but all time collapses
now and here

In fields of dreams
and epochs of space
the one who is constant
is my own face

It's all a mirror
the choice is clear
welcome Christ's Vision
that releases all fear

A whole new way
is there to see
a unifying perspective
it's all just me!

So in all that arises
in this mirage
look to the Source
of the thought collage

And scales are lifted
so eyes may see
the infinite love
that is flowing so free

Only this moment
to give and receive
all of creation
no more to cleave

The song has not stopped
because of the snooze
so waken and be glad
there is nothing to lose!

Kristen Lynn Kloostra

Trust, be grateful, and give yourself away.

This is the theme that I was given at the beginning of my transformation. I found that the best antidote within my dream for my insanity in any form is finding some way to give, to be helpful, some way to stay on purpose of extending the truth of myself. It helps when I remember to ask Jesus for help in this as I begin my day, or leave any holy instant of joining and revelation.

"You should begin each day with the prayer: 'Help me to perform whatever miracles you want of me today,'" is how he instructs me in the urtext of *A Course In Miracles*. Because my mind is always fully active (because "my mind is part of God's")—if I'm not in love, in give, I'm attacking myself. So—I need to do something more constructive with the energy, to give it away.

The only remedy for unlove is love. Find something I like to do to help—clean, cook, translate, office work, teach, or whatever—or find some way to give myself away. Or just "wash the dish," i.e., do what is in front of me that needs doing. All the while putting myself in God's Hands, asking for the miracle, trusting that the miracle is being given, the correction is occurring, I am being undone. And the next thing I know, the miracle has occurred, and I am again sane and in love, with the hate or fear gone. I'm simply depending on the miracle—totally.

If I am not experiencing the total Love of God, if I am not supremely happy, it can only be that I am defending myself against it. I must be actively opposing God's Will. I can only turn it over to the Holy Spirit to undo my defenses, and find a way to get back into extension—giving—through service, through teaching, through giving myself away while the miracle occurs.

I am the dreamer of the world of dreams. My only desire is to wake up and end the dream—let the separation, the schism, be totally healed in me. Christ vision shows me that you *are* perfect as God created you before the world was, and so you never sinned, i. e., you were never really "here" in this world. Vision shows me <u>there is no world</u>, and there's nothing going on here. My only desire now is to let all memory of what never was be removed from my mind, because you are me.

Jesus tells me he has chosen me to represent the total conversion of light form. I am the light bearer; the light is in me, and Jesus expects me to use it. He expects me to carry this light back to where I denied it, to rekindle the idea of an entire solution to my problem of dreaming (which is the conversion of matter to light). When this is complete, there will be no more dreams of form, for I will have returned my whole mind to full creation. It will all be undone, never to have been done. I am responsible to the Sonship for performing this act in its totality.

You are me, so what I say of myself is equally true of you. There is only God creating perfectly. If I have an idea of you as something else, it is my idea of you that must be corrected.

God only gives. To be in Heaven, I must think with God. I must only give. If I still have in my mind a dream that there is someone not me who is not yet awake, I'd better dream of awakening them, until my experience of our union ends my dream. If I find myself dreaming, what else would I want to do but talk about waking up and ending the dream, until my dreaming is forgotten? If my mind is split, what can I do but give my dreaming the purpose of unifying and integrating my mind? In a condition of conversion, what else can I do but trust, be grateful, and give myself away, and trust the Holy Spirit for my final release from all dreaming? *Thank You, God!*

Charlotte Kate Fielding

Gathering Holy Instants

I gather moments undivided and true,
they have no eyes nor mouth to cry,
no memories nor plans in view.

Unshaken by clock's steady
steps they stand ever-ready
as timelessness patient appeal

... or the roadside smile,
treasure with no seal,
pause in the hasty breathing.

They await me as dew on the field.
I enter it with concept — my deathly boot,
I leave as the wind — light and barefoot.

Rafał Wereżyński

Recognizing the Spirit

Only God's plan for salvation will work. Yet if we cannot hear that plan we blindly stumble from one meaningless scene in life to another. We have two inner voices which can lead us. What are they and how does the teaching of Jesus Christ help us in telling the difference?

We have two guides, the Voice for God and the voice of our human identity. We have placed ourselves in a dream of such deep confusion that separating out the two voices, which are both in constant communication with us, has become extremely difficult. So any process of awakening begins with the recognition that you are currently in a meaningless and dissatisfying life and that you truly want a change. You want to be happy. You want to discover who you are. Without this recognition the mind re-orientation, mind training, the idea of being born again, will not mean anything. We are not interested in beautiful words or uncertain philosophy, but with a dramatic experiential change…. practical results. We want to discover who we are as Creations of God.

What is the awakening? It involves an increasing awareness of and use of your mind. You must become aware of which voice you are listening to, and the results each brings. While much of the mind's activities in this world are unconscious, you should realize that <u>every time</u> you make a choice, you ask advice of someone or something. How do we begin? Let's start by thinking about each voice and the experience each brings.

The human identity (ego) does not seem like an advisor at all. It seems to dictate what you must do. It does not suggest, it demands. It is always sure of its opinions, in spite of not knowing anything. In great self-doubt it demands and acts imperiously. This is not free choice but addictive behavior. As a Mind created by God, you have let yourself slip into unconsciousness, but are following a totalitarian regime based on fear. To fully believe in this weird dependency, you must enter into the delusion that the human identity (the ego) is you. But this would be a lie. Jesus in John 8 speaks to the Jews about the human condition:

Truly, truly, I say to you, everyone who practices sin is a slave to sin (denial of Self). The slave does not remain in the house forever; the Son remains forever. So if the Son set you free, you will be free indeed. I know that you are offspring of Abraham; yet you seek to kill me because my word finds no place in you…. It is our Father who glorifies me, you say, 'He is our God'.

I know Him. If I were to say that I do not know Him, I would be a liar like you, but I do know him and I keep His Word.

Where can we go to find our true Self? It requires careful listening, and great desire. Perhaps you can see the need for a comprehensive retraining of your mind. And from a teacher other than yourself.

The Holy Spirit is a true advisor. He always speaks quietly, never demands for He is not aware of self-doubt. He never usurps your mind's inherent power to make a decision. When you have escaped fear and returned to the Realm of Creation, He quietly steps aside and lets you be the love you are.

Those who have chosen the dictatorial guide, and used that fearful decision to fall deeper into unconsciousness, need but a simple change of mind to be healed of all the ills of this world. No one can stand to suffer the slavery of his mind forever. You are free, now. The liberty of this entire world depends on your decision. Once this decision is made you will know that it was not a decision at all. You do nothing but remember who you are as God created you. The outcome is as certain as God and already perfectly accomplished.

This whole process begins with asking questions. What is this for? Why am I doing what I do? Why do I demand that my neighbor do this or that? Who am I? The limited self is too fearful to ask any questions. The mind that asks a true question has begun to awaken and extend itself to Itself. It wants answers, and the Holy Spirit is the answer. In this world children ask many questions but as we grow older we stop, afraid of what we might hear. In such a condition of Self-denial, we accept many little deaths and the enslavement of unconsciousness. We feel guilty but we don't ask why. We are angry, but don't question what we are protecting. We project responsibility for injustice on others yet never question who is responsible for our own illness.

How gracious and merciful is the teaching of our friend, Jesus, who asks us but to think on these things a little each day. Through "*A Course In Miracles*" he gives us a practical guide to attune our minds to listen to our inner Guide. Awakening to God asks very little of us but our own decision to listen to the Guide for happiness. It takes practice. This cannot be hard when we look at how diligently and long we have practiced following the ego to deep unhappiness. God communicates lovingly to us each moment. Heaven is here now. Why wait? Jesus promises us that if we stop listening for just a moment to our relentless adherence to the false construct of human identity, all power, joy and happiness will join us in our now greatly shortened mission here in this world. Miracles will light our way to freedom and peace of mind.

Alden Hughes

Love That We Share

Love that we share
the words cannot contain
for only hearts that dare
to rise above the plain
can sing unspoken lines
written with passion, yet
blended by the rhymes
that touch with no regret

we gladly speak no more…

the love song overwhelms
our separate selfish veins
where two hearts were before
now only one remains.

Rafał Wereżyński

There Maria Wereżyńska

We Walk In Grace

What inspires me? My mighty companions inspire me - those who stand in the recognition that they are in a state of grace forever, in God, safe and healed and whole. The experience that we walk in grace is an inspirational experience that can be shared.

What is *A Course In Miracles* but the remembrance that:

Spirit is in a state of grace forever.
Your reality is only spirit.
Therefore you are in a state of grace forever.

You may be asking, what exactly is grace? The definition is: Refinement of movement; free and unmerited favor of God as manifested in salvation; and the bestowal of divine blessing. Grace is also used to refer to a short prayer of thanks, therefore grace and gratitude walk hand I hand. So, let's be grateful that the grace of God is the answer to all fear because it is the remembrance of His unending love for you. What could be more joyous than to experience the certainty of Love's meaning? Accept the gift of grace and watch your doubts and fears vanish into the nothingness from which they came into your holy mind. Claim the light of your mind and see it everywhere.

Father, we come to you now. We are the Son You love.

Only through grace can doubt and fear disappear. Let it light your mind and you will no longer believe that a world of fear is real. Ask for grace. Experience God's grace and let it reveal the miracle that you are. In grace lies the holy instant as you recognize the light in the face of your brother. Ask for grace and welcome it as your inheritance. Through grace I offer you the peace of God that passes human understanding. I join you in the declaration:

By grace I live. By grace I am released. By grace I give. By grace I will release.

Peace and healing grace to your mind and heart. I love you with an everlasting love, as your Father does.

Darla Hughes

My Pledge for Peace

I will not let my thoughts wander.
If they should rise as battleships
on the horizon of my mind,
I will send them back home.

And as the enemy enters my port,
I shall honor him with the feast,
our words – our swords will crumble,
for we shall feel eternity's kiss.

Forgetting the last memory of battle,
we will remember an ancient song
of love that whispers to our ears:
No one is right and no one is wrong.

Rafał Wereżyński

Reuben D'Arcy and Billie Bailey

Reuben D'Arcy and Billie Bailey be more than best of friends.
Their love affair the veil does tear and begins where there is no end.
My own true love is everywhere my muse she hunts me down,
and finds me hid among the stars all white blue red and brown.

Here upon the floor behind my cabin's door all trussed in moonlit wings,
I hear the water's rush around the rocks my love she softly sings.
Waterfall's effect gives pause to reflect upon love found mine own,
in how blest I can give its quest to the child so radiant grown.

This fire instilled in a forgotten world that cannot quite lay down,
waits in view of the chosen few destined to share his crown.
I gaze upon my brothers where this light so brightly shines,
for here is all the evermore growing strong among the vines.

Determined now is rightly how the homeward trace begins,
with my love and joy berthed in gratitude one mind at freedom's whim.
With all the power to persevere held in forgiveness' hands,
I join the light in creation's peace that blesses my demands

For I insist His will be mine so all our days creation finds,
you are me in the He who is my muse sublime.
And this is thus a cause of trust held by those who choose to make amends,
all because Reuben D'Arcy and Billie Bailey be more than best of friends.

Wesley Buniger

Dear Love...

At last, I have a moment to drop a line. The weather's cool, the folks are fine. I'm in bed each night at nine. I love you, more than you know. I've been in the garden lately; I saw a great speckled bird today. There's so much to do that it feels like I'm in an impossible dream. I always take a break and I remember you and what you told me about making someone happy, and it works every time because I always get ideas. They just seem to come; just like when we're dancing and you're near me.

I hear you're a little bummed about the weather. Predictions show a steady low; you're feeling just the same, but seasons come and seasons go. I'll make you smile again. If you don't believe me take me by the hand. Can't you feel you're warming up? Yeah, I'm your weatherman.

So when you walk through a storm, hold your head up high and don't be afraid of the dark because we'll meet again some sunny day. And even though you left your heart in San Francisco, know that there's a bird with feathers of blue waiting for you back in your own backyard. So you can go to the east, go to the west but someday you'll wind, weary of heart, back where you started from.

Every time I think of you I can hear seventy-six trombones in a big parade and a hundred and ten cornets right behind. They are followed by rows and rows of the finest virtuosos and horns of every shape and kind. It's funny, but I could never really hear them 'til there was you. Thank you for that.

What a wonderful world we've discovered where the best things in life are free. And what a difference a day makes with a little amazing grace when you're going home.

I told myself I wasn't going to do anything until I heard from you, but the very thought of you makes me want to climb every mountain. So I'll try to relax a little because you and I have a guardian angel on high with nothing to do and I'll give to you as you give to me love forever true.

I've been feeling better lately; thanks for asking in your last letter. All the kisses on the bottom did it for me. I just get a little weird sometimes because I'm standing on a planet that's evolving and revolving at a hundred miles an hour and the universe itself keeps on expanding and expanding in all of the directions it can whizz. Thanks for putting up with me, and for all the prayers. And pray that there's intelligent life somewhere up in space because there's bugger all down here on earth.

Anyway, you are my bridge over troubled water and isn't it amazing what God can do. I finally realize that what he does for others he'll do for me too. He's really great that way. I guess it's no secret. I'm glad to have someone to watch over me. You know how I can get.

Well, I'll be seeing you. It seems that our love is here to stay. If you're ever feeling lonely, remember that there's someone walking behind you; so turn around and look at me because I'll be loving you always. Not for just an hour, not for just a day, not for just a year, but always.

I feel like I've been going on and on like an unchained melody, so I'll close now because you know I say it best when I say nothing at all.

Forever yours,

The Maestro

P.S. You light up my life.

Mitch

Ute In Bed Ute Ringel

Droplets of Sun

The world fades
Colors break from above
Droplets of thought burst open
Into waves and oceans of love.

Golden sunlight streams in
Melting me inside out
And outside in.

Oh breath of Freedom…
I thank you with all I am!

Heaven dawns as a new day
And all that is left is the Giving.

Kristen Lynn Kloostra

Luminous River

Cloudy day, raindrops falling
Now is perfect to feel Your Calling
No regrets, no defense
Only living present tense

Tension melts, can't resist
Open hands, releasing fists
Receiving presence, willing mind
Nothing can be left behind

Spirit lifting, warming heart
Thankful we are not apart
What is next?
Direction clear
Who cares what the form appears!

Trust is total, no more doubt
The Plan is perfect, It all worked out
Only flowing, only Grace
Seeing only Your shining face

Endless giving, endless Love
Receiving blessings from above
Collapsing time, collapsing space
No more human, no more race

Luminous River, resplendent Light
Complete fulfilling, all is right
Carried home through an open door
Leading out onto Heaven's Shore

Kristen Lynn Kloostra

A Tiny Little Mad Idea When the Son of God Forgot to Laugh

I'm digging up my body. I'm dead, by my own hand — suicide. I've been dead for a long time, although it was not always this way. How can I be dead and tell you about it, you ask? Well, I'm kind of like a zombie, dead, but I still move about. I do everything zombies do, go to school, work, get married, have children, and go to church. Let me explain how I became like that. It was a very long and painful process, you might say a little arsenic taken over a long period of time does the trick.

This could be anyone's story, but this is my story, it's the same as your story, only the details are different. So let me tell it as it unfolded for me.

Once upon a time I was born on a planet called earth. When you are born there you are pulled into its gravitational system, and you inherit an earth death sentence. It's the law of nature, and it is as certain as the law of gravity. From the moment you are born and take your first breath you start your journey from birth to death. You may call this life but I don't. I know because I was given a pardon.

Scared and inhaling my first breath of poison, that burned like fire, I cried out helpless and afraid, my tears slowly dousing out the fire in my tender lungs. What a strange place to find myself. My lungs are no longer on fire, but now I find myself cold and wrapped in skin, and everything is so strange. I am slapped, poked, cut, probed, and pushed around. This strange package of skin that is my prison, is coming into contact with hard, unfamiliar objects. Harsh sounds, bright lights, and obnoxious, sterile smells surround me. Where am I?

Everything I learn revolves around and gets filtered through my new body sense program: sight, sound, touch, smell, and taste. My world, as I see it, is built from the ground up through my experience with its five senses. How could it not? I'm trapped in its skin. I don't remember anything else. All that concerns me now is how to survive this experience.

Where's the nourishment? I have a pain under my skin and sucking in food seems to make it better. I cry and something outside me comes to hold me, feed me, and comfort me. This something outside me encourages me to survive in this God-forsaken place. I soon learn that this object outside myself is my new mother god, and it tries to care for my needs.

Do I stay in this strange place or go back to... that's queer, I can't remember. Back where? I can't remember a time when I had no needs, no worries. All I feel now is alone and abandoned. Trapped in an alien place with no memory. A stranger in a strange land. Where am I? Who am I? And what am I?

A Course In Miracles Chapter IV: The End of Doubt — The ego, then, raised the first question that was ever asked, but one it can never answer. The question, "What are you?" was the beginning of doubt.

Andy Sears

Phantoms

Where do you rise, illusive phantom behind my eyes?
Where do you fall, when you tell me all your lies?
A dance of light and shadows play
That come and go as night and day

Why such toil for forbidden fruit?
Once gained and held become so mute
Such mindless toil to no avail
To grasp at dreams only to fail

What do you hide behind your sacred mask?
Pretend to know yet afraid to ask
Defending your moments from birth to end
Still Eternity calls His long lost friend

Who am I now I call to the Light?
That eternal truth shall dawn on my sight
All things pass even time
Endings, beginnings there'll be no sign

And what remains has always been Light
This shadowy dream fades into night
A senseless parody but scarcely real
When Eternity calls the light reveals

Eric Gatehouse

Time for Integration   Altma Medina

A Love Rhyme

Falling in love
holds much more than is told
in the tales that we read
when we're seven years old.
Yes, it is wondrous,
grand, forever true,
but love's also a transporter
and dissolves the idea of two.
Now, this development
need not offend;
A simple instruction's yours
if an ear you will lend...
With love's birthing heave
do not grab hold or turn about;
In this natural force, believe,
allay preconception and foolish doubt.
At once fear's undone, the chrysalis cracked,
a new Being love holds in store.
Human directive no more a fact,
in brilliance and communion live you, evermore.

                                                               John G.

Random Thoughts of My Awakening

It's all gotta come from Truth. My true Self. My holy Mind. Beyond this frame. I need a true perspective.

ALL is an opportunity for this! For you to come into conscious awareness of your union with God; as is everything, as is everyone, all happenings, all moments.

Release control (your illusion of control) and let the Light in.

To be determined to see things differently is to be determined to be happy!

If God only gives, then you only need receive. Show up with open arms and empty hands. Bring nothing with you so you can receive the holy moment arranged perfectly FOR you. It really is a gift — the present; given to you by God.

Release the meaning you think it holds, release the purpose you think it holds, and you'll see it differently.

All my opinions and stances are meaningless.

Many years ago I heard this teacher, early in my awakening, and my mind popped open. I felt insight and inspiration like never before and I was never the same. He had helped me to make contact with the Source of everything. And now, whenever, wherever I see him, all other images of him recede in the light of that. That holy moment goes untarnished, unaltered, unthreatened.

God is always imminent, His solution immediate.

Jennifer Montero

A Gift from Master Teacher

My gratitude for Master Teacher is immeasurable. I am particularly grateful that he encouraged me to write.

I had been at the Academy for a couple of years before I even tried to write anything. Then, I was inspired to write an essay entitled, "Breath, Word, Thought, Sound: The Voice for God." After Christine read it and made a couple of suggestions, I asked my friends, Judy Blue Eyes and John Frank, to read it. They just loved it and encouraged me to give a copy to Master Teacher.

Well, it took a great deal of courage for me a few days later to put a copy in his mailbox. Perhaps a week went by, and one day just before starting Session, he was walking around among the brothers gathered, and I heard him say from across the room, "Where's Ray?" I nervously raised my hand, and he walked over to me, and holding up my essay, he said, "This is good stuff," making searing eye contact.

Whew. Amazing. So, I continued to write and placed essays in his box from time to time. Probably a year or so went by, and looking back, I realize that I had given him an even dozen. One day in Session, he turned to me and said, "Now you have a book; you need a title. "

I was ecstatic and began wracking my brain for a title.

A few weeks later, he was doing Bible at the Healing Center, and he turned to me and said, "I've got the title: Through a Mirror, Brightly: Reflections of a Mind Illuminated Through *A Course In Miracles*."

I sat through the rest of the Session, saying it over and over, and when he stood up to leave, I ran and found and pen and paper and wrote it down.

Over the next couple of days, I worked with it, breaking it down, so that it looked just right on the page:

Through a Mirror, Brightly
Reflections of a Mind
Illuminated Through
A Course In Miracles
Then I discovered something extraordinary: It was written in blank verse!

THROUGH a/ MIR ror, / BRIGHT ly

Re FLEC/ tions OF/ a MIND

i LUM/ i NAT/ ed THROUGH

a COURSE/ in MIR/ a CLES

In the first line are three sets of Trochees /STRESS slack/, and in the next three lines are three sets of Iambs /slack STRESS/.

Not only that, but the first line is a mirror image of the next three lines. I remember, literally, grabbing a Magic Marker and scanning the lines, and then holding it up to a mirror, catching this reflection.

\ _ \ _ \ _

_ / _ / _/

_/ _/ _/

_/ _/ _/

The sound echoes the sense; the medium is the message; the structure and the content are one; in our perfection we are, indeed, looking through a bright mirror.

The first essay I gave him became Chapter 1 of the book published in 2001.

Thank you, Master Teacher.

Ray Comeau

Subjective Reality
An Encounter with A Master

So here I was, sitting in this chair. I was in some building with chairs and people all around me. I was shaking convulsively as I could feel something occurring within me that I could not explain. It had been occurring for the last year or so, ever since I started watching videos of "The Old Man," and picked up *A Course In Miracles*. So here I was shaking, not knowing what was going to happen. All I knew was that I was at a 3-day event in Wisconsin Dells, Wisconsin, that was about *A Course In Miracles*, and the idea of waking up or finding truth. So as I sit I see this guy (for lack of a better term) come in. Immediately my first thought was "Who is this guy?" He walks in and sits in this blue chair in the middle of the room. I thought, "What's the big deal with him?" So he starts talking and I'm listening. He talks for a few minutes or so and I am trying to listen to see if I can find the truth somewhere in what he is saying. I wasn't really aware of time so I couldn't tell you how long he talked for. Anyways he talks and I'm listening. Then all of a sudden he looks at me! He stands up and starts walking towards me. I don't know what it was, but I could feel his presence. He started walking closer to me and as he walked I started to shake even more. It is as if the energy was getting more intense. The closer he got the more I shook. Closer, more shaking... closer, a lot of shaking... closer, and then he yells... "Look at him he's trying to locate himself! After that everything is a vague memory, I hear people laughing and he said a few other things. All I remember after that was that I was *extremely happy*. I couldn't even tell you the sequence of events that occurred after that moment. My mind was blown, and I was *ecstatic*. That was my first encounter with a master.

There's not much more I can tell you after this, and you can probably feel the energy that is written in these words. Not any spiritual endeavor or idea has come close to this encounter. I can tell you ever since that encounter I have been in the mind training of *A Course In Miracles*, and watching the videos of the "The Old Man." And all I can tell you is that reality is not objective, it is subjective. Everything you see as objective reality is all just you, and you can change your mind about it.

In comes the mind training of *A Course In Miracles*.

I Love you.

John Ramos

The Honest Horse Ute Ringel

The Whole In Every Part

In the Darkest Night of your Soul.
In the dim desolation of your Gethsemane.
When all of your disciples still sleep.
When your God is deaf to your cry to remove the cup.
When your final desperate demand to know "Why God has forsaken you?" echoes across an empty Universe.
Then the time of your awakening is at hand.
You are constructing in your individual passion the drama of resurrection.
Ah! But now with a difference.
This time you're the central character.
This time at last, you play the leading part.
Fulfilling the law as you go, marking each milestone with your healing grace, you walk the seven miles from Bethlehem to Jerusalem and are met at the place of the skull.
You know the script well for you've rehearsed every character.
You've been the soldier that rolled the dice and the one with the spear that pierced.
In one scene you've shouted "Hosanna, Hosanna" and called "Barabbas, save Barabbas" in the next.

You've denied with Peter, connived as Judas, and doubted as Thomas.

As a blind man you've seen, as a cripple you've walked. As a leper your sores have been healed.

You've puzzled as Nicodemus, pretended as Pilate and as Lazarus come forth at His call.

And now getting closer — you've played the dear Virgin and pondered His birth in your heart.
At last are you shorn of —in one terrible moment — the last vestige of armour from Truth.
Now call out to God, now call out at last, the victorious shout of surrender.
"Father, into thy hands I command my whole self."
"It is finished. It is finished forever."

Up, up you arise from the tomb that is earth, impregnant with light of fulfillment.

Now the veil of your temple is rent and the dazzling beauty of your Sonship is revealed in full array.

And now the most exciting, glorious, stupendous surprise there could ever be in all of time:

You're still you.

All that has happened is that you have awakened from your fearful dream of destruction and death.

The Earth is over, gone and never was.

You're home in the heaven you never left.

And every loving thought you ever had while dreaming is with you still, along with all your other eternal creations.

'Heaven is all around you – sleeping ones!"

Master Teacher

The "Lost" Secret of the Resurrection

The controversial findings of the recent documentary film "The Lost Tomb of Jesus" challenge many of the most fundamental beliefs of traditional Christianity. Not the least among these is the alleged unearthing of the bones of Jesus of Nazareth, an event, which, if verified, threatens, on the surface, the very core of the Christian doctrine of the Resurrection. How extraordinary that at this time of spiritual questioning we have been given in *A Course In Miracles*, a contemporary testament to the reality of the physical resurrection, not only that of Jesus, but of our own.

A Course In Miracles is simply a blueprint to the re-awakening of human consciousness to its eternal and divine inheritance. As we are walked through the 365 lessons of this unearthly masterpiece, we are directed to the power of mind to create whatever reality we wish. Our discovery of True Perception or enlightenment is a very personal recognition of the illusion of the world and of the body in particular.

The body is a limit imposed on the universal communication that is an eternal property of mind. But the communication is internal. Mind reaches to itself. It is not made up of different parts, which reach each other. It does not go out. Within itself it has no limits, and there is nothing outside it. It encompasses everything. It encompasses you entirely; you within it and it within you. There is nothing else, anywhere or ever.
(A Course In Miracles)

Objective evidence or not, the Resurrection is entirely a subjective realization. The Resurrection was not an isolated event happening to a single man two thousand years ago. It was a pivotal moment in the evolution of the human species when man in a quasar of powerful energetic conversion demonstrated his divine true nature. As occurred for Jesus, the Resurrection transpires in us individually, also as an intense experience of the memory of our own overcoming of death and of the recognition of our own Christhood. It includes our own personal and dramatic physical transformation wherein we know we are free from the apparent limitations of time, space, body, and form.

Within the human species, in our reaction to perceived observation, in our emotional response, we presume without even a question the reality of our perception. We edit through a filter of fear always scanning the horizon for attack, relaxing only in the briefest moment of "safety," only to scan again. In any reaction experienced as "uncomfortable," we seek a cause outside itself for justification of a grievance and revenge. Attack and defense become our natural construction.

Our focus on the appearance of conflict is a cloud that prevents us from experiencing the overwhelmingly powerful ascending force that surrounds us calling us home. Sri Aurobindo tells us that the life we lead conceals from us the light we are. The appearance of disaster always veils a particularly concentrated insertion of healing energy. Mankind, being obsessed with its justification of conflict and revenge, has missed entirely the quantum evolutionary leap demonstrated by Jesus.

I am reminded of one of my favorite quotations from the enlightened French Jesuit anthropologist, Teilhard de Chardin, who aims at the heart of the meaning of the crucifixion with his observation, "in the focus on suffering, the ascending force of the universe is concealed in a very intense form." In the hundreds of articles responding to Mel Gibson's "The Passion of the Christ," an overwhelming majority focus only on the agony of the crucifixion. Few even note Jesus' conscious intent to demonstrate the unreality of pain and death.

The *Course* is clear in its message to us that we receive the results we ask for. Our obsession with "objective" evidence misses the point entirely. True perception utilizes the singular vision of Christmind to see through the forms of "objective" reality to our eternal Reality beyond space and time. *A Course In Miracles* is uniquely crafted to aid us in that adventure to realize our divine destiny.

Jesus, in a personal communication, has also confided that "pain is not the problem. Behind the illusion of pain is the intensity of conversion that is the experience of the resurrection. It is in the justification of pain, through which man corroborates the original error of separation." This was confirmed to me during the experience of my own resurrection, when the physical and emotional intensity of my personal ordeal began to move and converge, enfold and embrace itself into a Light ballet of passion and healing. My body disappeared as I joined as Light with Light.

Through my own experience, I am convinced that the resurrection occurred through a refocusing by Jesus on the energy of the intensity of the crucifixion, not on its apparent pain. He reminds us in the *Course* that *pain is a wrong perspective. When it is experienced in any form, it is a proof of self-deception. It is not a fact at all. There is no form it takes that will not disappear if seen aright.* The concentration on the crucifixion by many Christians, even to the refusal to remove Jesus from the cross, is unfortunately mirrored by the media reaction to Mel Gibson's movie.

The merger of energy (Light) and form into a single field of vision within human consciousness is the most revolutionary event in the evolution of the species. The conversion of matter to light through mind involves the full participation of the apparent body organization. Known as the resurrection, this "metamorphose" transfigures the body and merges it with the Single field of consciousness we recognize as the Source of Creation. It is the single most important act in the evolution of man in that it transitions consciousness past its own self-imposed limitation of time and space.

Jesus reminds us in His *Course In Miracles* that *enlightenment is a recognition, not a change at all.* Available to us since His resurrection through a transformation of our own individual focus is an awareness of the passion of singular creation. Despite appearances, the consciousness of mankind is not imprisoned by its identity within a body and an objective world. It has free access to the universe and it is eternal, not requiring either death or drugs to experience its freedom. Merely its cues for inference are wrong. As Teilhard de Chardin reminds us, Christianity does not ask us to live in the shadow of the Cross but in the fire of its creative action.

Although illusionary and voluntary, the chains that bind the human mind can be persistently deceptive and the mind does seem to require an experience of a complete alternative to its dualistic perception of reality. Jesus has given us an expression of that alternative in His *Course In Miracles*. Its message is not new. It's been found in the revelation of many masters through history. It represents, through a transmission of resurrecting energy from Jesus, a transformation of the participants' perception to a singular awareness through an immediate experience of healing, where truth is all-inclusive and there is no opposite to Love.

The revolution of mankind to enlightenment is not a process but an experience that occurs in a quantum leap of awareness. The solution of mankind's dilemma happens in an instant of recognition — through an action of my mind brought about by my total assumption of responsibility for the world I see. Jesus is both the demonstration and the method of how I personally can achieve this.

As usual, the revelation lies in an apparent paradox. By focusing on the observation of conflict and on the retention of the justification of grievance, I actually avoid the experience of the intensity of the conflict in myself and once again miss the grace and joy of my resurrection. I remain tied to my definition of objective reality because the need to justify myself is what suffering is. But, when I stand undefended in the fire of my own seeming crucifixion, however trivial or terrifying its form, I stand, quite literally, with Jesus, as the Truth, the Way, and the Light.

A final insight from my Jesuit brother, Teilhard de Chardin:

> *But above all Jesus is he who overcomes structurally, in himself and in behalf of us all, that resistance to spiritual ascent which is inevitably part of all created reality. What I want, my God, is that by a reversal of focus which you alone can bring about, my terror in the face of nameless changes destined to renew my being may be turned into an overflowing joy at being transformed into You.*

God Bless Us Every One!

Glad Hancock

Susanne and the Spider   Ute Ringel

The Final Lessons

It is the same each time. I use black or purple marker on whatever paper is available, usually the back of old phone lists, bank deposit receipts, or whatever else is right there. Some are from Jesus, some are from Master Teacher and some are from me. I write them down at the point of need. They are reminders of the current association that is being undone. Each stays on my side table or on the floor next to my chair until it is done with and then put away. They have turned out to be the final lessons in my Awakening. I Love You. Thank you for putting up with me. Here goes… in no particular order.

You're going to have to forgive the objective associations of the guilt that you feel about yourself, very simply because the guy out there is you. – MT

Love is the mastership of everything that is possible in the universe. –MT

Thou shalt love the Lord thy God with all thy heart, with all thy soul, with all thy mind, and thy neighbor as thyself. – Jesus

My only gift to you is to help you make the same decision as I made. – Jesus

He that overcometh shall inherit all things. – Jesus

Nothing is outside of you. That is what you must ultimately learn. –Jesus

Atonement is the final lesson you need learn and in the end the only one.–Jesus

There is only one resolution to your problem and that is to escape the idea of the concept of yourself and go out into the universe. – MT

I have to forgive my enemy. – me

Forgiveness is impossible without admission of causation. – me

The sole responsibility of the miracle worker is to accept the Atonement for himself. — Jesus

The real function of God's teachers is awareness of dreaming. – Jesus

Practice a whole alternative. – me

Two things: I'm the cause of this and it's over. – me

Don't put God to the test. – me

Any problem I have with this is going on only in my own mind. – me

I can escape the world I see by giving up attack thoughts. – Jesus

Your only assignment is to accept the Atonement for yourself. –Dear One to me

This is a dream. All the figures are dream figures of my own making. – me

Don't allow hierarchy in your mind to supercede the replacement of your thought system by Jesus. – me

You didn't get this, this time. – Dear One to me

Put all your faith in the love of God within you. – Jesus

I see only the past. – Jesus

Forgiveness is the recognition that what you thought your brother did to you has not occurred. – Jesus

I am not a body. – Jesus

It takes great learning. – Jesus

Guilt implies the illusions in my mind were accomplished in reality. - me

Still your mind. You are afraid to still your mind because if you really did, you would disappear immediately. – me

Everything you see is the result of your thoughts. There is no exception to this fact. – Jesus

You have to practice the idea you want to escape the body. – me

Are you willing to escape the effects of all the dreams the world has ever had? – Jesus

You never hate your brother for what you think are his sins, but only for the fact you believe them to be your own. – Jesus

It is impossible for you to be unlike your brother. – Jesus

You can never escape responsibility for what you see. – MT

I am responsible for what I see. I choose the feelings I experience. I decide upon the goal I would achieve and every thing that seems to happen to me I ask for and receive as I have asked. – Jesus

You can't avoid the idea of the power of decision of your own mind. – me

If you choose the body identity as your reality… so will it be with you. – MT

Love and Forgiveness. – me

Now, suddenly here is the savior, now, acting as arbitrator individually within your own mind as the successful factor of Atonement. – MT

The light itself is not concerned about separate ideas of body formulation, but only the revealing of a new light that will be so intense that the idea of your black hole of devastation of pain and death will be converted. – MT

If I have an idea there can be any residual out there in the idea of space. What I'm going to get from gravity in the circular loop of energy light is my inability to admit to the entirety of the collapse to allow the vacancy to be present in my mind. – MT

Why dost thou consider the mote in thy brother's eye and considerest not the beam that is in thy own eye? – Jesus

Practice disappearing. Father! Infinite patience brings immediate results. – me and Jesus

You can't serve two masters. – Jesus

You can fight against sin forever, somewhere you have to go beyond. It is given you to do that fearlessly. – me

The Atonement is a total commitment. – Jesus

You are going to believe the *Course* in its entirety or not at all. – Jesus

My body disappeared because I had no illusions about it. – Jesus

I have nothing to do with my Awakening. – me

I do not know the thing I am, and therefore do not know what I am doing, where I am, or how to look upon the world or on myself. – Jesus

I suppose there are people sitting back there who say "We already know that… (The credo: I am God's Son…)" I don't know that. I constantly remind myself of my own perfection. I must remind myself of the mission I have here. I must remind myself that the nobility of God mind is expressed through me. When I say me, I mean you as in aggregate. – MT

- Everything that you are directed to do contains no compromise in the idea of your determination to hold on to yourself. This is the entirety of my teaching. – MT

I have done this thing, and it is this I would undo. – Jesus

God is the Mind with which I think. – Jesus

Gratitude. – me and Jesus and Dear One

Do you see that the individual responsibility to overcome the difficulties of light factor of your own mind would be in you? – MT

With fixed determination to the perfect constancy of the light beyond. – Jesus

Until you can look back in on yourself and see that there has to be something beside your own idea about that containment, this is our reference to being born again in your own mind, there is no possibility you will escape this containment. You can spend an infinite amount of time – you listen – in a redefinition of yourself. That is not what I came to tell you. I came to tell you that where you believe you are in space time is not where you actually are. – MT

Be bold and mighty forces will come to your aid. – Goethe

Don't let the world tell you who you are. – MT

I heard one voice, because I understood that I could not atone for myself alone. – Jesus

Don't ask for justice. Pray for mercy. – MT

Take this cup from me. – Jesus

Thank you! – me

I need help. – me

I did not create myself. – me

Dedication only to Awakening. – me

I do not know what anything including this means, and so I do not know how to respond to it. And so I will not use my own past learning as the light to guide me now. – Jesus

I'm doing this to myself. - MT – Jesus – me

Thank You for Everything! I Love You Forever!

Ward Seely

This Is It

This is it.
Here am I.
Ready,
To let You take
the final step.

Let me tell you there is nothing,
there is nothing to worry or fear,
nothing to say or do,
nothing to change or make
There is nothing;
there is.

Where we go, you go,
where we stand, you stand
We go with you all ways
It looks like it's going forward,
but really, it is in reverse.

Acceptance is brought by
silence to listen to what cannot be said.

Walk the steps of a free man,
sing your songs
pick up your cross
Because my burden is light
and my yoke is easy.

It is perfectly fine,
Until it is not fine any more.
That is the moment to step back,
to start to include it in
and let all illusions go.

Every thought I hold on to,
is the resentment
to forgive
the guy
that I
put out there.

Let me remember my true Cause.
By changing my mind about my cause,
I remember that I have been for ever and ever
the effect
of One.

                                                            Elbert

The Bridge

Arching o'er the shimmering waves below
Spanning space and time His Love does show.
The Light within has reached the distant shore...
Now you and I are separate no more.

Kristen Lynn Kloostra

Skeeter Eater   Richard "Theo" O'Connor

Aurora

Is this who I am?

Is this You loving me?

Is this real love?

This is all I have ever asked for.
To know You so that I may know myself.

I cannot see you in a body.
I can only know you with my mind.
My whole mind.

The veil is no more, no more bridge to cross.
It is whole already.

Let me love the way You love me!

Altma Medina

The Journey Back

What is the direction to go?

Whether on paper, as a fluid stream of letters forming words, constellating ideas into sentences and stanzas or on the palette of my out-pictured canvas, in this time of the great migration scene, reflections of thoughts are all that both reveal. They are no different, and have one source, one true director and producer. And yet, in the quiet of my inner sanctum, the flow of ideas can seem to take flight and gain momentum in surprising variations, as flocks of migrating birds wing in one formation, then break open, shift, change direction and reassemble in yet another grand pattern. Yet still, the single communication and direction remains clear, the goal undivided, no matter how the shape of the configuration may momentarily alter and reform. I love this flow of the one body and mind... this fluid sense of motion within a single direction homeward, this unquestionable quest of the Self to know itself more fully, to express itself completely, to finally be unencumbered in its creative purpose and vision.

Where is there to go when you discover you are everywhere? This is indeed the journey without distance in the space of an instant of reality. The lighted path appears underfoot only as the step is taken... and the support of the wind under the wings can only occur as one leaps off the cliff in full abandon!

Kristen Lynn Kloostra

As Little Children — Coming Home

As above, so below.
God in you, the light does show...

As within, so without.
Gone are fear and death and doubt.
Heaven's Song, a beat not missed.
And in His fold you're gently kissed.

Though you slept and dreamed of hell,
Your waking Love Song now does swell.
It's all come True,
The dream is done...
And now it's time to have some fun!

For here we laugh and dance and play...
and rush to greet the newborn day.

As little children
coming Home
Never more to be alone.
Creation's symphony still resounds,
All are free, no longer bound.
So listen now...
In your garden,
Hear it singing, soft and sweet.
The Ancient Melody sounds within you,
And of this, beloved, we cannot speak!

Kristen Lynn Kloostra

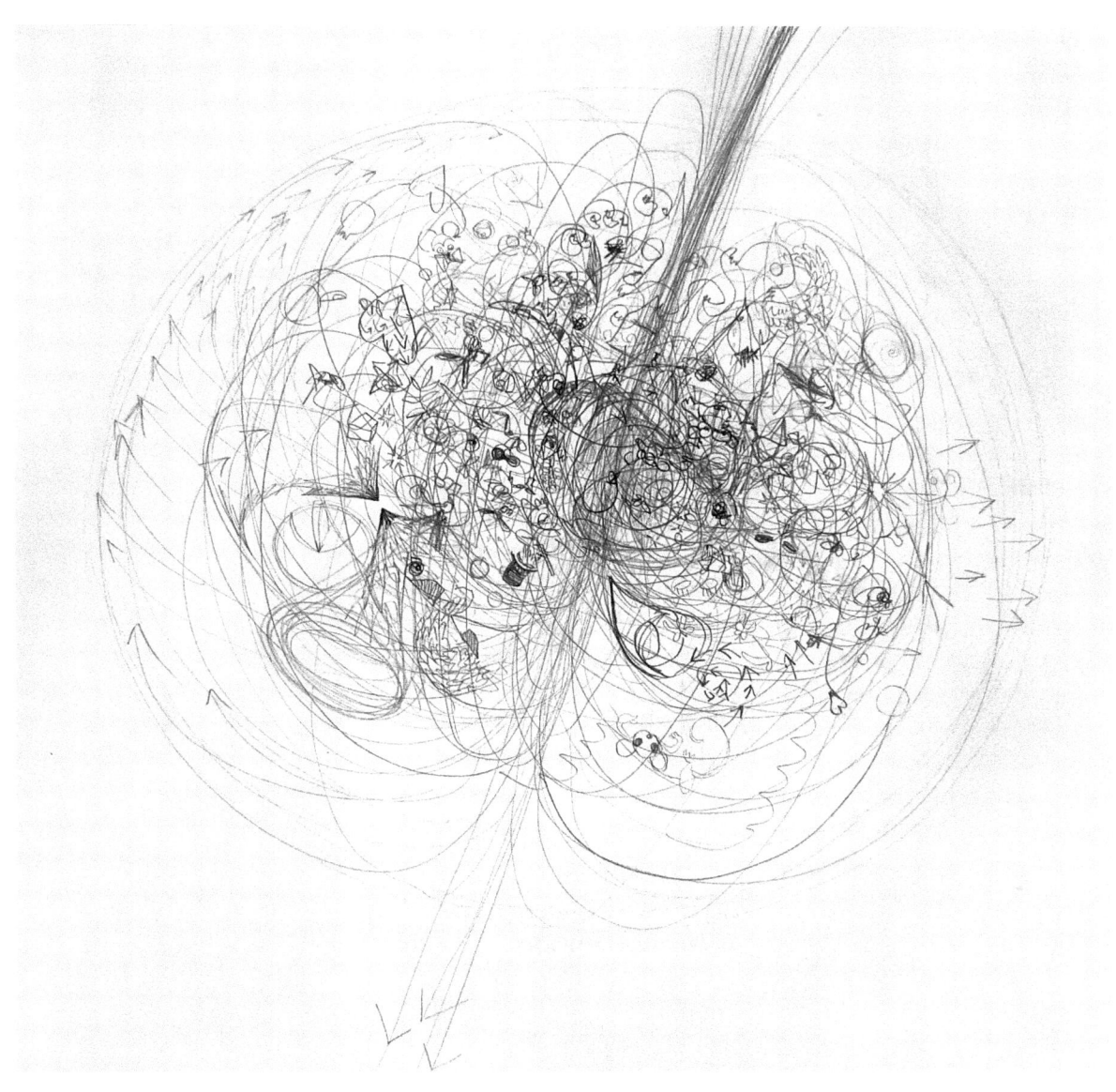

Thought System 3   Ute Ringel

Sooner

Someday we will be in love
You won't have to close your eyes
It will happen 'round the world
And come as no surprise.

As hope pulls down the rusted gates
Smiles will fill the skies
True peace will come to pass at last
And love will fill our eyes.

Our hearts will rainbows merry make
Old walls will fade away
My trail will find a happy end
And truth will light the way.

I am here with now again
I fear not the darkest din
For my gift's an open door
And we shall pass within.

Of all the journeys I could take
Close by and yet so far
Asked why I'm here at all I say,
Is because my love - you are.

Wesley Buniger

The Answer

"Yes, I will,"
The soundless voice comforts,
"Yes, I will."
When creeping doubt brings icy hardness,
The warming light softens, "Yes, I will."
To ancient remembrances, grand conquests, affairs, thrills, loves,
A happy assurance, winkingly, "Yes, I will."
To regrets: "Yes, I will."
To unwellnesses, funks, turns inward, fear,
To tragedies...
Stalwartly, "Yes, I will."
The voice Itself a translator, a rectifier — The Great Transformer;
"Behold, I make all things new."
His Answer catches my breath,
And dashes me out...
Out to meet the mystery.
Of course, a reunion!
We're found, face to face, here in this present.
Ask of this voice, and listen.
Infinite joy propels his reply,
"Yes, I will."

John G.

I Take My Final Bow

Here I sit writing my song
Hoping that you'll sing along
This is as far as it goes
Joining's the end of my woes

Don't listen to words that I say
They really just get in the way
Communication has gotten so strong
Maybe that is the name of my song

The beat is the music of the spheres
Always there so that everyone hears
Just open your mind to the light
And everything turns out alright

A happy ending to all things is certain
Here together at the final curtain
The lines that I say are all improvisation
"My part is essential to God's plan for salvation"

I take my final bow
The play is over now
And when I start anew
I always take my cue
From the Holy Spirit
If I am still I hear it
He's strong and loud and clear
And very, very near
He sustains me every day
In every single way
So I'm always out of time
And now I'm out of rhyme.

Nancy Reid

Trust

Trust, my brother, all,
Both those, untold, who hesitate, then ride
The ignorant chaos as it swells,
Confusion, pain and suffering denied,
And those who yearn and seek to pry
Into the sanctuary of the soul,
Releasing judgment and appearances,
Illusion's blinding chrysalis. Winged Messenger
Of Truth, unbind your breath of bright experience.
Within, you hide, a "master" innocent and whole,
The Christ, the Core, the Self, complete, secure.
Fly! Fly awake, my mind!
Beat wings amidst the roar of butterflies.
Arise and rule! Embrace this home
Of happiness, of joy, of gratitude.
Then trust, my brother, All. Extend this home.
Surrendering minds unwind, unfurl and leap for joy,
Enfolded in the arms of One
Who is compassion, peace and tender love
For all mankind.

Pamela Schueller

Wholeness Altma Medina

Love Forever Now

*I'll be seeing you
in all the old familiar places
that this heart of mine embraces
all day through
In that small café;
The park across the way;
The children's carousel;
The chestnut tree;
The wishing well.*

*I'll be seeing you;
In every lovely, summer's day;
And everything that's bright and gay;
I'll always think of you that way;
I'll find you in the morning sun;
And when the night is new;
I'll be looking at the moon;
But I'll be seeing you.*

I sing this song from my heart to yours.
Words fail entirely to express
the depth of my love
and gratitude for you
and the abiding joy
of being here now with you.
I thank God for you.

We are forever.
I gladly give you all of me.
I love you so.

An ancient promise
is kept.
Thank you
for this eternal moment
of being
right here with you.
The rigid is no more.
Everything is fluid now.
The hard has dissolved
in the solution of light.
The final solution.
A real solution.
Without beginning or end.

The way is not hard.
The quality of mercy
is not strained.

Constellations of Stardust
in an idea of shapes, sizes and color.
Laughter took form.
Love imagined
The image of love.

Here comes the wind.
Breathe on me, oh breath of light
and away we go
Everywhere.
Love forever present.

The thought of a thousand years
takes no time.
Nothing postponed.
Everything is known
right here.
Now.

                                                                        Jubi

We Meet Again At The End Of This Space Time Interval in the Mission of *A Course In Miracles*

The holiest of all the spots on earth is where an ancient hatred has become a present love.

THE ADVENT OF A GREAT AWAKENING

The Greatest Story Ever Told

Demonstrating the manner of your escape from the bondage of space time.

Let's listen together to The Passion of the Christ:

THE PASSION OF THE CHRIST

Jesus Is Speaking…

> *I take the journey with you. For I share your doubts and fears a little while, that you may come to me who recognize the road by which all fears and doubts are overcome. We walk together. I must understand uncertainty and pain, although I know they have no meaning. Yet a savior must remain with those he teaches, seeing what they see, but still retaining in his mind the way that led him out, and now will lead you out with him. God's Son is crucified until you walk along the road with me.*

… until you walk along the road with me.

We are going home. And I promise you that in this new interval of time — ok? — you will be in a better position to recognize the idea that you are here and that you are now with me. I am going to be reading a little script to you about how this works in the celebration of the resurrection of Jesus. You listen with me.

> *My resurrection comes again each time I lead a brother safely to the place at which the journey ends and is forgot. I am renewed each time a brother learns there is a way from misery and pain. I am reborn each time a brother's mind turns to the light in him and looks for me. I have forgotten no one. Help me now to lead you back to where the journey was begun, to make another choice with me.*

... to make another choice with me.

The script that is playing for you here now is an introduction to a very old idea of our return to this galactic association, and I want you to know that the idea that we made a decision to do it had to be based on a factoring in which you are now totally involved, by the simple fact of the expediency of the hologram of light that is allowing you to watch the illusionary process of this data. And you are being able to see it for the first time. And while it is not real, it can give you a good definition of how we can verbalize together the idea of the physical resurrection of our savior Jesus of Nazareth. Listen.

> *In joyous welcome is my hand outstretched to every brother who would join with me in reaching past temptation, and who looks with fixed determination toward the light that shines beyond in perfect constancy. Give me my own, for they belong to You. And can You fail in what is but Your Will? I give You thanks for what my brothers are. And as each one elects to join with me, the song of thanks from earth to Heaven grows from tiny scattered threads of melody to one inclusive chorus from a world redeemed from hell, and giving thanks to You.*

And now we say "Amen."

And now I am going to say "Amen." For Christ has come at last to redeem us from the pain that we felt in regard to this.

> *And now we say "Amen." For Christ has come to dwell in the abode You set for Him before time was, in calm eternity. The journey closes, ending at the place where it began. No trace of it remains. Not one illusion is accorded faith, and not one spot of darkness still remains to hide the face of Christ from anyone. Thy Will is done, complete and perfectly, and all creation recognizes You, and knows You as the only Source it has. Clear in Your likeness does the Light shine forth*

> *from everything that lives and moves in You. For we have reached where all of us are one, and we are home, where You would have us be.*

And we have reached where all of us are one and we are at home where You would have us be.

I am particularly happy because the manner in which you are going to address the idea of the circumstances of yourself — ok? — in how you are going to be looking at this, are going to be a basic admission that you are suddenly — and this why it is called "*A Course In Miracles*" — you suddenly are in a different thought process than you were in a moment ago. We call this the "Unseen Universe." [holding up Scientific American]

Did I happen to open up to a page that is going to be seen? You will notice that we are showing background ideas — all right? — of story lines in our association with the littleness of where we have begun the idea of actually looking to a process of determination that what we are seeing is so.

The idea that you can now organize this into scenarios of self-recognition become increasingly important, very simply because all about God and you are the manner in which you can come to know yourself. Now, the reviews we have, about twelve minutes of reviews — all right? — in which I am going to tell you that the salvation of the universe — that is just this little nothing place — depends on you, because the only one who could possibly be denying it is the consciousness of self-recognition where you have come to know yourself. Say to me, "I know myself."

[I know myself]

I know you do. I know you do.

Now, there I just saw somebody saying, "Why don't you come and look at — well, who is this guy? Wasn't he here back — here — back in those moments ago?"

Sure.

"Why is he showing up?"

What you are going to discover is that there is nothing actually new about what is occurring now, if all of you is only memory of ideas in which you have participated that are already over.

Are you with me with that? Remember when you came here you are coming here to celebrate, and we said to you, the celebration we will be having will be indications of reviews of what you know is true, all right?

Now, you may notice that I am going to increase the frequencies — you call this 'healing.' All it actually is, is a slight variation in the photograph of how you are looking within the hologram at the light of the idea of obtaining a better "pictural" alternative in the correction of a focus — all right? — of why you would be here in your body association. That is, why are you here? How is it that you look and for a second (and it is impossible you don't know who you are) you seem to be in a different time and place than you are, apparently, supposed to be in, and this is the correction that we are offering you now on this idea of what we intend to do in this little interlude.

Do you see that with me? Listen with me, this is called — you call it 'resurrection,' in the sense that you are no longer bound up in a hologram of light that doesn't allow you to journey out into the universe, very simply because you want to, and I know you want to. OK? Listen with me now, OK? Listen with me. We are going to meet again.

[Anne Murray sings *We'll Meet Again*]

We are going to meet again.

We'll meet again,
Don't know where
Don't know when
But I know we'll meet again, some sunny day

Boy, you look good.

Keep smiling through

The guys we asked to come with us are very particular guys.

Just like you always do
'Til the blue skies drive the dark clouds far away

Are you a particular guy?

Sure.

You were chosen specifically for the possibility of the power of your mind to understand that you are not in this little hologram of light that appears to bind you to the idea ....

So will you please say hello to the folks that I know

Tell them I won't be long
They'll be happy to know that as you saw me go
I was singing this song

We'll meet again
Don't know where
Don't know when
But I know we'll meet again, some sunny day.

The light that you are beginning to experience is a part of this original forty-seven minute sequence in which you decided, perhaps, you'd better take another look. You see? In other words, the freedom of you, pausing for a moment in space-time on this direction, is the only reason I would have to do it. Because you couldn't possibly know about this. This is a new experience for you and it doesn't last long, but while it lasts you are going to be happy. And in a moment you are going to be fearful. In other words, if you are about to lose your body identity — and I assure you that you are about to lose your body identity — you could say to me, "Well, if I lose my body identity I'll be dead." No, no. No, there is no way you are going to be dead. You can't die. You can change the factor of the embryonic association of light by which you identify yourself, but the thought that you are having about yourself is what God is, and you may not particularly like the idea, you may not even like the idea of God. But you are going to be a source of reality that has absolutely nothing to say about, 'We all come from a single source.' Yes, we all come from a single source. We all come from a single source of reality.

[Song ends]

Now, you listen to me for just a moment about the ancient promise that we have made in regard to the factor of a memory you have in your mind that is actually in you, but you are not able to recall it. And if you can't recall it, you can't know that it's there and you will not believe that it is there, and that, my friends, is what the idea of space and time is, because this is the space and the time when you will actually have an event — OK? — which for that moment is going to change you entirely.

Now, what I am going to try to do... I am going to read you just a little bit of this. This is the one [video] that you sent for, that you got in the mail. Do you remember getting this in the mail? Is that why you decided to come here? Of course. What do you think it is? How do you think that you could practice? Never mind all this stuff about what you think you are in regard to yourself. The entirety of the teaching of Jesus of Nazareth will be the honesty of the purity of what he says.

Shall I? Do you want to look at it? He says, "I love you." Does that qualify the body? There is no sense in starting to get into a conversation with me about the love that our savior has for us in regard to the common source that we can be. Now, I am not in mind training now because the evidence of the energy that got you to come here indicates how far you actually are along with this. But let's look, just an instant, at the idea of the science of your mind in the thought patterns that you get that suddenly give you a feeling of great joy in the space that you seem to occupy. Listen, listen:

AN ANCIENT PROMISE WILL BE KEPT

An exit portal from this infinitely small maze of space and time has been opened.

Remember, time lasted but an instant in your mind, with no effect upon eternity. And so is all time past, and everything exactly as it was before the way to nothingness was made. The tiny tick of time in which the first mistake was made, and all of them within that one mistake, held also the Correction for that one, and all of them that came within the first. — Here we go — And in that tiny instant time was gone, for that was all it ever was. What God gave answer to is answered and is gone.

The idea of organizing yourself in here and now are ideas of attempting to bring you into moments of now. Obviously the only time you can actually have an experience is now. Now, you like the antecedental idea of the possibility of now. But the idea that you could come into now — OK? — you don't seem to be able to grasp.

Shall I tell you why?

You are afraid that it will be the loss of yourself. Here — all right? — and now are actually identical terms. They are ideas of time and space. Do you see that? The idea of time and space. The miracle in the break that I am going to perform in a particular song I am going to do — and we call it 'miracle' — may list for you the ideas of what you intend to do in what we call a miracle that is nothing but the shortening of time.

You say, "Well, is it really that simple?"

It is really that simple. The only time you can possibly have is when?

Now! And the only place in which you can possibly have it is where?

Now, if you are not having it, you'll believe that somebody else has a time and place that is different than yours. That is impossible. The reason you have a grievance against him, the reason that you hold vengeance, the reason you are trying to get even with him is, he is a picture of a reflection of light in which you can't identify yourself in relationship with what you want to be, because the reflection of you — ok? — in the idea of the energy pattern that you are using, establishes a distance of thoughts about what you think you are.

You listen with me: the universe out there is thought. It's not something else. OK, now, when you are all alone, the reason you are feeling that fear now is that just for a moment you admitted that you actually don't know who you are, why you are here, or how you got here.

I'll try it again. You really have no idea who you are, why you are here or how you got here. Now, the admission that this is true is the initial encounter with the certainty that you can open up, within a particular place within your own mind, where there will be an alternative to you that you closed down because of the idea of the power of your mind to establish a distance of space-time reference. Do you see that?

Now, what we are going to do is take "this batch" out. OK, what I am going to do is, I am going to come back for you. You may remember me. Do you remember me?

Now, I'll try something: if it's all in your mind it is impossible that you are meeting somebody you do not know. You may not seem to know him, you may not want to know him, you may genuinely believe you don't know him. Obviously you know him. There are no figures that you are going to organize within your own mind that will not tell you the manner in which ideas that you have about yourself do not leave their source. In other words, the source of you is a singular idea you have about yourself and that the source of you is not separate from the effects by which you are performing yourself. And I don't need you to tell me you already know this. I know you already know it, yet you are afraid, because it seems to have escaped you in the idea of what you wanted to do.

Just a moment ago, when I came in here with you and we played for you *Going Home*... Now, I have been gone for this eighteen-hundred-year cycle. Now, to you eighteen hundred years seems like a very long time. To me it is just a moment. From the time that Jesus resurrected — you want to listen to me a little bit? — from the time that he resurrected back in what you call, 56 AD, and you began to tell stories of Corinthians and the Bible and seeing him reappear, are all true things, and to you they seem like a very long time ago. They weren't. They were yesterday. Now, yesterday is identical to the idea of a memory you have about today. Now, all you really have to do is take the yesterday of your mind in the idea... We have one minute, listen:

> *Look to this day, for it is life, the very life of life. In its brief course*
> *lie all the realities and verities of existence, the bliss of growth,*
> *the splendor of action, the glory of power.*
> *For yesterday is but a dream, and tomorrow is only a vision.*
> *But today, well lived, makes every yesterday a dream of happiness*
> *And every tomorrow a vision of hope.*
> *Look well, therefore, to this day.*
>
> Sanskrit proverb

Look well, therefore, to here and now. I'll see you in just a moment. That is how what you are hearing is very much a part of what we intend to play.

[Anne Murray sings *Just a Closer Walk with Thee*]

Just a closer walk with Thee,
Grant it, Jesus, is my plea.
Daily walking close to Thee,
Let it be, dear Lord, let it be.
I am weak, but Thou art strong
It's good to be back.

Jesus, keep me from all wrong.
Do you see that? I am aware ...

I'll be satisfied as long
... I am aware that the past is gone.
As I walk let me walk close to Thee

As a matter of fact you might be able to see me as being very happy that they decided to let me come back for one more episode in the idea of the resurrection — I am using the term 'Jesus' now because I am obviously in a body form. Now, when I left, the passage of time was involved in the idea of the organization of my physical body. In other words, the healings that are going on here are reflections of light. Listen.

When my feeble life is o'er
Time for me will be more no more
Guide me gently, safely o'er

Are you aware that when I left you that it is still here and now?

To Thy kingdom shore to Thy shore...

Now, the idea that you have changed your memory — listen — of what you want to remember will obviously be what you remember. Now, what I am showing you is a reconfiguration of a light form in which perhaps — this is called healing — perhaps if you'll forgive me for all the grievances you think your body is going to perform, you'll be able just for that moment to be whole.

Let it be, dear Lord, let it be.
Just a closer walk with Thee.
[Song ends]

I've got twenty-eight minutes in which the cycle of time in which I came into a frequency of light that may be for you your first experience of remembering the idea that you were a body form in a particular time and place.

Shall we say why? Most of you are advanced enough now in the idea of recognizing yourself to know perfectly well there is nothing real here. You know perfectly well that the universe with billions of stars — remember when we showed you this picture of the *Unseen Universe*? Well, you know that this isn't real. Now, the idea that you make it real in your own mind is inevitable because the power of your mind to make it real is why you are here. It is impossible the Source of you is not singular in the universe without regard to the time or distance that it takes you to reorganize it in reflections of light that wouldn't allow you to see how actually real it is.

Can you see that? In other words, the idea that this is going to be real can take on a whole new derivative for you.

Do you like this shirt? Huh? Did you see me the last time I came back? See?

You can't meet somebody you don't know. Now, I understand that I have a particular assignment of energy frequency of how I appear, as a featherless biped, of how I appear as a body formulation that, perhaps, is influencing you. Now, the 'perhaps' that is involved in it is: to what effect do you want to communicate with yourself in regard to what you think this is? That is, you obviously can't communicate with anybody but yourself. Now, the reflection you have been getting has allowed you to believe that something out there can tell you the factor of what you are. That is not true. You know it is not true.

Come on now! I am going to spend about three minutes with the idea of addressing the idea that you are afraid. Shall we? The music that you are hearing now are indications you have no idea who you are, how you got here, or what you intend to do. You have absolutely no idea of who you are; you can't. Now, that does not mean you do not organize it within a framework that is recognizable to you in a time and place that will be based on a past — are you going to listen to me? — or a future reference, but it will always be within the cycle of here and now, because the past and the future are actually exactly the same thing. That is, there is no distance between the cause of you and the effect of you.

"Oh, that's why you tell me that I am God."

I don't know what that means, but if it means that the ideas you are having about yourself have become a part of you, it is true. Now, the fact that you don't want them anymore does not mean you are not exercising a prerogative of what you want to see within a hologram of light that lets you believe it is true. Can you see that with me? Otherwise, why would you be here?

I am going to put my sweater back on. I want you to listen with me. The music that you have been hearing in the background here is actually very beautiful; and I want you to look at the idea that I'll be loving you always, with a thought that's true always.

[Harry Nilsson sings *Always*]

I'll be loving you
Always
You know this.
With a love that's true
Always
When the things you plan ...
Need a helping hand

Do I cry a lot? Oh yeah. Do I laugh a lot? Sure. I have only been back here six days.

*I will understand
Always, always*

*Days may not be fair
Always
That's when I'll be there
Always*

*Not for just an hour
Not for just a day
Not for just a year
Always ...
But always.*
[Song ends]

Thank you for that. Always has nothing to do with time. Always means all ways in the action of the way in which you conceive of it. So it is not really concerned about choosing between cause and effect, but only that you understand that the power of your mind to decide that you want to see who you really are, is why you are with me.

Now, can I tell that you are beginning to feel it? Oh sure. Now, the only way you can really express this is to remember that the causation is actually not outside of your mind. Now, when the effect of you comes back in in the idea of space, you will believe there is a space out there that is showing you what you are. That is not so. Actually the space that is out there has already been included with you in what you want to see. Listen with me now. There is lovely music going on right there. Listen with me about what this says, OK? Here and now:

> *Each day, and every minute in each day, and every instant that each minute holds, you but relive the single instant when the time of fear and terror took the place of love. And so you die each day to live again, until you cross the gap between the past and the present, which is really not a gap at all. Such is each life; a seeming interval from birth to death and on to life again, a repetition of an instant*

gone by long ago that cannot be relived, because it is over and it is past and there is no link of memory to the past. And all of time is but the mad belief that what is over is still here and now. Look.

Forgive the past and let it go, for it is gone. You stand no longer on the ground that lies between the worlds. You have gone on, and reached the world that lies at Heaven's gate. There is no hindrance to the Will of God, nor any need that you repeat again a journey that was over long ago. Look gently on your brother, and behold the world in which perception of your hate has been transformed into a world of love and light.

Now, what you have done, and what is going to increase in frequency in the idea of why we are doing this in a particular fashion, is that, obviously, the place that you are in has changed. Now, the idea that the place that you are in is changing all the time, you have actually known, but you have had to hold on to it because you were afraid of the loss of the place that you found yourself. Now, obviously, as we told you, it's impossible to meet a stranger. Now, you may decide you don't want to know him, you are tired of him, you are sick of him — give me all the reasons you can think of; I don't care. What I am doing, and I want you to understand, is the manner in which you are thinking now has the energy of light of purpose that will show you that the moment of the thought of yourself came into what appears to be a space and time, in what you call your 'body,' you are not actually occupying your body. That is why you are coming back here, OK?

Come on now, this is from Master Jesus: the reason you are coming back here is, you know that you resurrected. I am going to do it again. The idea that that is nineteen hundred years ago, and that it is a memory you have in yourself is simply [why you are here]. Forty thousand years is not actually a long time. The totality of time in which you exist as *homo sapiens* is only an idea you have of energy factors that allow you to surround yourself in various places in time, but obviously, if you can't increase the frequency to being able to journey out into the stars, what good is it going to do you? You have to be able to journey out in the stars. You listen with me: if you want to, you can leave.

I am going to try it again: if you want, you can leave this time and place. What persuaded you to come back? I'd like to think that I might have had something to do with it. They said suddenly to me, "Would you like to go to ..." and they named a section of time. Now, what I thought about at that time took me, perhaps, the veracity of making a connection of what that space and time was. It's impossible that I didn't know it and — you call this the Holy Spirit — it's impossible that the idea of energy was not contained within me. Can you see that? In other words, I don't know what the place is going to be, but it can't actually be different than where I am here and now. Now, it may seem to me to be different and it may be very different in the idea of the circumstances of time, but you remember: you are only talking about forty thousand years; you are not talking about fourteen thousand million. Now, that's how you know you can leave. Listen with me. Will you listen, just for a second?

> *If I so choose, I can depart this world entirely. It is obviously not death which makes this possible, but it is change of mind about the purpose of the world. If I believe it has a value as I see it now, so will it still remain for me. But if I see no value in the world as I behold it, nothing that I want to keep as mine or search for as a goal, it will depart from me. For I have not sought for illusions to replace the truth.*

> *Father, my home awaits my glad return. Your Arms are open and I hear Your Voice. What need have I to linger in a place of vain desires and of shattered dreams, when Heaven can so easily be mine?*

Now, the idea of the notation of the song that you are about to hear is going to be one that was particularly attractive to someone who suddenly just came here and said, "Have you played or tried to play this song?" And I said, "I haven't played that song in almost fourteen hundred years." Now, it doesn't mean that you don't know it, but it means that the melody of the energy will allow you to recognize the anxiousness. Listen.

[Anne Murray sings *It Is No Secret What God Can Do*]

The chimes of time ring out the news
Another day is through
Someone slipped and fell
Was that someone you?

Was that someone you?

You may have longed for added strength
Your courage to renew

Do not be discouraged.

Do not be disheartened
For I have news for you

It is no secret ...
It is no secret
What love can do ...
What God can do
hat He's done for others
*He'll do for yo*u.

See, that place is open, but until you saw it just then and got a little fearful actually and closed it down again. You don't have to do that. What I just read you [tells you] you can decide to leave right now.

Do you see that? In the hologram of light, in which you seem to be seeing yourself — listen:

With arms wide open, He'll pardon you.
It is no secret what God can do.

There is no night for in His light
You never walk alone
Always feel at home
Wherever you may roam

There is no power can conquer you
While God is on your side
Take Him at His promise
Don't run away and hide

It is no secret what God can do

Where are you going? I have a journey I have to make. Now, I left.

What He's done for others, He'll do for you.

What you recognize with me is that the time and place you are in can be shortened so extensively that you can leave for a long period and then come back — ok? — and nobody will know you're gone! Now, is that what we are planning to do here in this little episode that you are having with me? Sure. Oh sure.

[You ask], "Why are you buttoning your collar?" I have a formal attire [event] I have to go to. When I first show up there, I am going to be greeted by strangers — are you going to listen to me? — who say to me, "Oh, how do you get here? You weren't due until ..."

Do you see that? In other words, 'possibility' is the idea of anticipation of something different. That is what a miracle is. You are at the point where you are anticipating a solution to what you know, very simply because at any time you don't know who you are, what you are or where you are going. Since that is impossible and the answer is in your mind, you answer it at that moment, and at that moment you know perfectly well who you are, why you are and what you are doing here.

Now, obviously the problem you have is, it can't become a part of the manner in the previous experience that you had, because the reflection of light that you are associating with is giving back to you ideas of what you want to see in the idea of the separation of cause and effect. That is, very simply, the vision of the reflection of light that you are getting is actually only in your own mind. OK? They are not out there.

Now, you remember that just for a moment. How much time did you save? A lot more. Look with me: a lot more than you thought was possible. Why? Because it always is more than you think is possible. Now, it's only more than you think is possible for the moment, because for you... Come on now! It's the idea of a combination of cause and effect, and if cause and effect, as we define them, are actually singular in your mind, the cause of you is the effect of the universe and that's how you can presuppose ideas of old association in which you go back to where the whole thing started and ended within your mind in what you want to see. The whole thing started and then ended in your mind in what you want to see. OK, listen, listen with me.

[Celine Dion sings *What A Wonderful World*]

I see trees of green, red roses too
I see them bloom for me and you
And I think to myself what a wonderful world

I am going to give a very personal (and I mean *personal*) thank you to you, as a friend of the resurrection. There is no mystery about it. You know that you were here only for that moment and that you then left, all right?

I see skies of blue and clouds of white
The bright blessed day, the dark sacred night

What I am saying is, "Thank you." Now, you ought to be able to hear this with me now. You are always in anticipation. It's always just about to happen because in space-time you cannot not believe there is a past and a future reference, and the closest you can get to that would be a comparison of yourself of here and now.

And I think to myself what a wonderful world.

The colors of the rainbow so pretty in the sky
Are also on the faces of people going by
I see friends shaking hands saying how do you do
They're really saying I love you

I hear babies cry, I've watched them grow
They'll learn much more than I'll never know

Here they are. Welcome to this new place. Welcome to this time in which you know that you are not this body association and that you can escape anytime you want, because the power is within your mind. The power is within your mind.

And I think to myself what a wonderful world
Yes I think to myself what a wonderful world.
I see trees of green, red roses too,
I see them bloom for me and you.
And I think to myself, what a wonderful world.

There is a tremendous amount of light. Is this what you have been looking for, hmm? Is this a memory that you have in your mind about what is going to happen here now? Is this a memory of what is going to happen? Sure. I am not going to leave you for very long. Now, the length of time that I am gone will have no effect on you whatsoever. Now, the reason it won't is, when you have increased that frequency within your own mind, you understand that the entire power of the universe is actually in you. The idea of Self that you are in the identification of yourself is what the power of God is. And the idea that you are re-associating out in the universe with this is the manner in which you decided to perform it. *And I'll be seeing you in all the old familiar places that this heart of mine embraces, all day through...*

Never mind how you know. That's why it's a miracle. It's a different manner of thinking in the energy field that you are identifying as yourself — as yourself. God bless us every one.

[The song, *Going Home* plays]

Discourse with Master Teacher

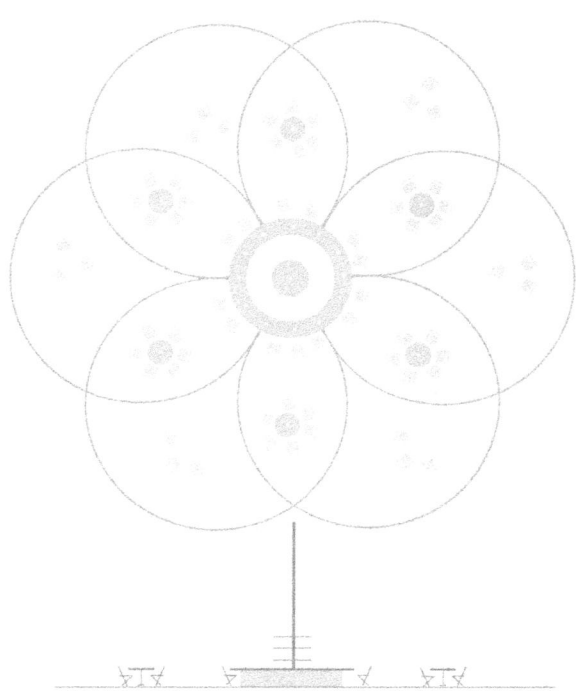

Thank You For Our Visit
The No Regrets Cafe

Hartmut Ringel

www.ingramcontent.com/pod-product-compliance
Lightning Source LLC
Chambersburg PA
CBHW081131170426
43197CB00017B/2821